Mainstreaming Gender in World Bank Lending

An Update

Other Titles in the Series

PREPARED BY THE WORLD BANK OPERATIONS EVALUATION DEPARTMENT

Poland Country Assistance Review: Partnership in a Transition Economy
(1997)*

Agricultural Extension and Research: Achievements and Problems in National Systems
(1997)*

Fiscal Management in Adjustment Lending
(1997)*

Reforming Agriculture: The World Bank Goes to Market
(1997)*

Paddy Irrigation and Water Management in Southeast Asia
(1997)*

1995 Evaluation Results
(1997)*

Zambia Country Assistance Review: Turning an Economy Around
(1997)*

Aga Khan Rural Support Program: A Third Evaluation
(1996)*

Lending for Electric Power in Sub-Saharan Africa
(1996)*

Industrial Restructuring: World Bank Experience, Future Challenges
(1996)*

Social Dimensions of Adjustment: World Bank Experience, 1980-93
(1996)*

1994 Evaluation Results
(1996)*

Ghana Country Assistance Review: A Study in Development Effectiveness
(1995)*

Evaluation and Development: Proceedings of the 1994 World Bank Conference
(1995)

Developing Industrial Technology: Lessons for Policy and Practice
(1995)*

The World Bank and Irrigation
(1995)*

1993 Evaluation Results
(1995)*

Structural and Sectoral Adjustment: World Bank Experience, 1980-92
(1995)*

Gender Issues in World Bank Lending
(1995)*

The World Bank's Role in Human Resource Development in Sub-Saharan Africa: Education, Training, and Technical Assistance
(1994)*

1992 Evaluation Results
(1994)*

New Lessons from Old Projects: The Workings of Rural Development in Northeast Brazil
(1993; contains summaries in French, Portuguese, and Spanish)

World Bank Approaches to the Environment in Brazil
(1993; contains summaries in French, Portuguese, and Spanish)

Trade Policy Reforms under Adjustment Programs
(1992)*

World Bank Support for Industrialization in Korea, India, and Indonesia
(1992)*

Population and the World Bank: Implications from Eight Case Studies
(1992)*

The Aga Khan Rural Support Program in Pakistan: Second Interim Evaluation
(1990)*

*Contains summaries in French and Spanish.

Mainstreaming Gender in World Bank Lending

An Update

Josette Murphy

The World Bank
Washington, D.C.

Manufactured in the United States of America
First printing June 1997

Cover: Children in rural Guatemala. Photo by Curt Carnemark, The World Bank.

Josette Murphy is a senior evaluation officer at the World Bank.

ISSN 1011-0984

Library of Congress Cataloging-in-Publication Data

Murphy, Josette.
Mainstreaming gender in World Bank lending : an update / Josette Murphy.
p. cm. —(A World Bank operations evaluation study)
Includes bibliographical references (p.).
ISBN 0-8213-3981-8
1. World Bank—Developing countries. 2. Women in development—Developing countries. 3. Investments, Foreign—Developing countries. 4. Economic development—Developing countries. 5. Economic assistance—Developing countries. 6. Loans, Foreign—Developing countries. I. Title. II. Series.
HG3881.5.W57M873 1997
332.1'532'091724—dc21 97-17870
CIP

Contents

Foreword

A 1994 study by the Operations Evaluation Department (OED) traced how the concepts of women in development and gender had evolved within the Bank and how Bank policies and lending reflected these concepts. At the time, few projects with gender-related actions had been completed and evaluated. Bank management and members of the Board's then Joint Audit Committee requested that OED update its work on gender as more information became available.

This update seeks to confirm or revise—based on a larger body of evidence—the 1994 study's preliminary findings, and to review progress in implementing Bank policy and OED recommendations in recent lending and nonlending work. The review incorporates evidence from a total of 802 projects with gender-related actions approved in FY67–96, focusing in particular on the results of 58 projects for which outcomes have been evaluated. It analyzes the overall quality of lending in FY94–95 for gender integration, compares it with that of completed projects, and reviews recent economic and sector work and country assistance strategies.

The update shows that some excellent work is being done, in line with Bank policy and the recommendations of the first OED study. Three findings are particularly encouraging:

- Projects with gender-related actions achieved their overall objectives more often than similar projects without gender actions approved in the same years.

- Projects that explicitly incorporated gender goals into the main project objectives were the most likely to achieve their gender objectives.

- The design quality of gender-related actions in projects approved in FY94–95 showed a significant improvement over the design quality of gender activities in completed projects approved during FY87–91.

The review also indicates that gender work may reinforce and benefit from other initiatives—such as increased use of social assessments—to make social development a key element of the Bank's strategic agenda. The most pressing need is for more projects and country assistance strategies to systematically address gender issues. The update calls for actions to ensure that gender concerns are addressed in ongoing work on social assessments, performance indicators, and guidance for implementation completion reports. It recommends that gender-related research be expanded and deepened, and that monitorable targets for implementing gender action plans be developed. Last, the study calls for each sector to identify priority goals and targets related to gender, and specifically, to promote greater coordination and synergy across the Bank in this critical dimension of development.

Robert Picciotto
Director General
Operations Evaluation

Prólogo

En 1994, el Departamento de Evaluación de Operaciones (DEO) llevó a cabo un estudio para determinar la evolución que habían tenido en el Banco los conceptos de participación de la mujer en el proceso de desarrollo y de género, y la manera en que éstos se reflejaban en las políticas y operaciones de financiamiento de la institución. En la época en que se realizó el estudio se habían terminado y evaluado muy pocos proyectos que incluyeran actividades relacionadas con el género. La administración del Banco y los miembros del entonces Comité Conjunto de Auditoría del Directorio Ejecutivo pidieron al DEO que actualizara su labor sobre la problemática del género a medida que se dispusiera de más información.

En la presente actualización se procura confirmar o rectificar —teniendo en cuenta un conjunto más completo de datos— las conclusiones preliminares formuladas en el estudio de 1994, y examinar los avances en la aplicación de la política del Banco y de las recomendaciones del DEO en las recientes operaciones crediticias y no crediticias. En el examen se tienen en cuenta los datos de un total de 802 proyectos que incluían actividades relativas al género aprobados entre los ejercicios de 1967 y 1996, prestándose especial atención a los resultados de 58 proyectos sometidos a evaluación. Se analiza la calidad general del financiamiento otorgado en los ejercicios de 1994 y 1995 en lo que respecta a la incorporación de las cuestiones relativas al género, y se la compara con la calidad de los proyectos terminados; se examinan también los recientes estudios económicos y sectoriales y las estrategias de asistencia a los países.

En la actualización se señala que la labor que se está realizando es excelente y que está en consonancia con la política del Banco y con las recomendaciones formuladas en el primer estudio del DEO. Cabe destacar tres conclusiones especialmente alentadoras:

- De los proyectos aprobados en los mismos ejercicios, la proporción de proyectos que incorporaban actividades relativas al género y que alcanzaron sus objetivos generales era mayor que el porcentaje de proyectos que no incluían tales actividades.

- Cuando las metas relativas al género se incorporaban explícitamente a los objetivos principales del proyecto, las posibilidades de cumplirlas eran mayores.

- Se observó un mejoramiento considerable de la calidad del diseño de las actividades relativas al género de los proyectos aprobados en los ejercicios de 1994 y 1995 con respecto a la de los proyectos terminados aprobados en los ejercicios de 1987 a 1991.

En el examen se señala también que la labor relativa al género puede reforzar y sacar provecho de otras iniciativas —como el mayor uso de las evaluaciones sociales— para convertir al desarrollo social en un elemento fundamental del programa estratégico del Banco. Urge que en más proyectos y estrategias de asistencia a los países se aborden sistemáticamente las cuestiones relativas al género. En el documento se recomienda tomar medidas para asegurar que la problemática del género se incluya en las evaluaciones sociales en curso, en los indicadores de resultados y en la orientación para los informes finales de ejecución. Se recomienda, asimismo, ampliar y profundizar las investigaciones relativas al género, y establecer objetivos que puedan supervisarse para la puesta en práctica de los planes de acción sobre esta problemática. Por último, en el estudio se pide que cada sector establezca metas y objetivos prioritarios relativos al género y, específicamente, que promueva una mayor coordinación y sinergia en todo el Banco con respecto a esta dimensión esencial del desarrollo.

Robert Picciotto
Director General
Evaluación de Operaciones

Avant-propos

En 1994, une étude effectuée par le Département de l'évaluation des opérations (DEO) a montré comment la notion de rôle des femmes dans le développement et celle de parité hommes-femmes en sont arrivées à être incorporées aux politiques et aux opérations de prêt de la Banque. À l'époque, un petit nombre de projets comportant des mesures relatives à la parité entre les sexes avaient été menés à bien et évalués. La direction de la Banque et les membres du Comité mixte d'audit du Conseil ont demandé que le Département de l'évaluation des opérations mette à jour ses travaux sur la parité des sexes au fur et à mesure que l'on disposait de nouvelles informations sur la question.

La présente mise à jour a pour objet de valider ou réviser les constatations préliminaires de l'étude de 1994 sur la base d'un ensemble de données d'expérience plus vaste, et d'examiner les opérations récentes, de prêt et autres, afin de déterminer si des progrès ont été accomplis dans la mise en oeuvre de la politique de la Banque et des recommandations formulées par le DEO. L'étude porte sur 802 projets au total comportant des mesures relatives à la problématique hommes-femmes approuvés entre l'exercice 67 et l'exercice 96 et analyse plus particulièrement les résultats de 58 projets dont les résultats ont été évalués. Elle examine la qualité globale des prêts pendant les exercices 94 et 95 du point de vue de la prise en compte de la parité des sexes dans les opérations, établit une comparaison avec la qualité des projets menés à terme, et passe en revue les stratégies d'assistance aux pays et les travaux économiques et sectoriels plus récents.

Il ressort de cette mise à jour qu'un excellent travail est accompli et que l'évolution est conforme à la politique de la Banque et aux premières recommandations formulées par le DEO. Trois conclusions sont particulièrement encourageantes :

- Les projets comportant des mesures relatives à la problématique hommes-femmes ont atteint leurs objectifs généraux dans une proportion plus importante que les projets qui concernaient des secteurs analogues approuvés au cours des mêmes exercices mais ne comportaient pas de mesures relatives à la problématique hommes-femmes.

- Les projets qui intègrent des buts liés à cette problématique dans leurs objectifs principaux sont ceux qui ont le plus de chances de les atteindre.

- La qualité des mesures relatives à la parité des sexes s'est sensiblement améliorée pour les projets approuvés durant les exercices 94 et 95 par rapport aux projets approuvés entre les exercices 87 et 91 et maintenant terminés.

La mise à jour indique également que les activités concernant la problématique hommes-femmes peuvent renforcer d'autres initiatives — comme par exemple les évaluations sociales — ayant pour but de faire du développement social un élément clé de stratégie de la Banque et que ces activités peuvent en être elles-mêmes renforcées. Il est impératif de faire en sorte que davantage de projets et de stratégies d'assistance aux pays incorporent systématiquement les questions relatives à la parité des sexes. La mise à jour préconise un certain nombre de mesures visant à assurer la prise en compte de ces questions dans les travaux en cours sur les évaluations sociales, les indicateurs de performance et les rapports de fin d'exécution. Elle prône l'élargissement et l'approfondissement des travaux de recherche sur la parité des sexes et la fixation d'objectifs vérifiables qui permettent de suivre l'exécution des plans d'action dans ce domaine. Enfin, l'étude recommande que chaque secteur précise ses buts et objectifs prioritaires et s'efforce en particulier de mieux coordonner les activités menées dans l'ensemble de l'institution et de faire jouer les synergies à l'appui de cette dimension clé du développement.

Robert Picciotto
Directeur Général
Évaluation des opérations

Acknowledgments

This update benefited from the comments and suggestions of many people in the regions and central vice presidencies. Special thanks are extended to Aysegul Akin-Karasapan, Lynn Bennett, Mark Blackden, Jayati Datta-Mitra, Monica Fong, Christopher Gibbs, Roslyn Hees, Alcira Kreimer, Caroline Moser, Minh Chau Nguyen, Manuel Peñalver, Sheila Reines, Roger Slade, Cecilia Valdivieso, and external reviewer Mayra Buviníc. The participation of 43 staff members in focus group discussions is also gratefully acknowledged. Within OED, Nalini Kumar and Varsha Malhotra contributed extensively to the review and analytical work, Emily Chalmers edited the draft, and Megan Kimball and Carla Sarmiento processed it. Angie Gentile-Blackwell copyedited and produced the published version.

Abbreviations and acronyms

AFR	Africa regional office
CAS	Country assistance strategy
CIDA	Canadian International Development Agency
CODE	Committee on Development Effectiveness
DAC	Development Assistance Committee
EAP	East Asia and Pacific regional office
ECA	Europe and Central Asia regional office
ESW	Economic and sector work
FIAHS	Fund for Innovative Approaches in Human and Social Development
FY	Fiscal year
GAP	Gender Analysis and Policy team
HRO	Human Resources Development and Operations Policy Vice Presidency
ICR	Implementation completion report
IDA	International Development Association
LAC	Latin America and the Caribbean regional office
MIS	Management information system
MNA	Middle East and North Africa regional office (formerly MENA)
MOP	Memorandum to the president
NGO	Nongovernmental organization
OECD	Organization for Economic Cooperation and Development
OED	Operations Evaluation Department
OPR	Operations Policy Department
PCR	Project completion report
PHRWD	Women in Development Division, Population and Human Resources Department
PREM	Poverty Reduction and Economic Management Network
SAR	Staff appraisal report
SAS	South Asia regional office
UN	United Nations
WID	Women in development

Summary

Objectives and methods

In 1994, an Operations Evaluation Department (OED) study (later published; see Murphy 1995) traced how the concept of women in development, and later the broader concept of gender, came to be reflected in Bank policies and lending. That same year, the Bank issued a policy paper, the Operational Policy 4.20, and a best practice note, which called for integrating gender concerns in Bank work. This update of the 1994 study has two objectives: (1) to confirm or revise the preliminary findings of the 1994 study, drawing from a larger body of evidence; and (2) to review recent lending and non-lending work for evidence of progress in implementing Bank policy and OED's 1994 recommendations.

The update draws from an independent review of existing documentation, including project documents and files, related economic and sector work, and OED evaluations. It includes discussion of the results of 58 projects with gender-related actions approved in FY87 or later and closed by December 30, 1995.[1] This update also examines the integration of gender into the objectives of 120 projects approved in FY94 and FY95 and analyzes the characteristics of all investment lending with nominated gender-related actions approved in FY94, FY95, and FY96—a total of 185 projects. Lastly, the update reviews the gender content of selected sector work. Bank staff contributed through focus group discussions and individual interviews. Bank management provided OED with a report on the implementation of the ledger of recommendations from the 1994 study.

Main findings

Bank-supported projects with gender-related action achieved their overall objectives more often than did projects without

Projects with gender-related action achieved their overall objectives—that is, received a satisfactory outcome rating—in relatively greater proportion than projects similar in sector and year of approval but without gender actions (Chapter 2).

Seventy-four percent of 54 completed projects with gender-related action approved in or after FY87 in the agriculture and human resources sectors were rated satisfactory for overall outcome, compared with 65 percent for the 81 projects with similar sectoral distribution that did not include gender-related action.

Projects that explicitly incorporate gender goals into the main project objectives are the most likely to achieve their gender objectives (Chapter 2).

Regression analysis confirms the 1994 finding that gender objectives are achieved more often if they are well integrated into the main project objectives, rather than contained in a separate component.

The design quality of gender-related actions improved significantly for projects approved in FY94 and FY95, compared with completed projects approved between FY87 and FY91 (Chapter 3).

Two-thirds of recent projects with gender-related actions included a substantial or high level of gender analysis, compared with only 16 percent in completed projects. Over 70 percent of recent projects integrated gender considerations into overall project objectives, compared with about half of the completed projects. Participatory approaches and a higher quality gender analysis were often found together.

But there is still substantial room for increasing the proportion of projects and country assistance strategies (CASs) that systematically address gender issues (chapters 3 and 4, respectively).

The prevalence of projects with gender-related actions remained around 30 percent of the investment portfolio in the last three years. This is below the peak of the early 1990s, which began to approach the 45–50 percent level—possibly a realistic upper bound. Coverage in CASs, as stipulated in Operational Policy 4.20, remains uneven. Coverage in implementation completion reports (ICRs) is sparse.

Conclusions

Gender work may reinforce—and benefit from—other initiatives to make social development a key element of the Bank's strategic agenda

This update shows that some excellent work is being done and that progress has been in line with the recommendations made by OED in 1994 (Chapter 1). Regional offices have produced interesting initiatives, and gender action plans are being completed. The high standards and commitment of many staff, both those who work explicitly on gender and task managers, are exemplary. The finding that projects with gender-related actions are associated with satisfactory achievement of their overall objectives reinforces the current policy of mainstreaming gender in Bank operations. Senior management and the board are providing strong leadership on gender issues.

The update also indicates that gender work may reinforce—and benefit from—other initiatives to make social development a key element of the Bank's strategic agenda. These initiatives open powerful avenues to mainstream gender in Bank work by linking gender analysis and social assessments, including gender among factors that identify relevant stakeholders, and when appropriate, making sure that performance indicators measure results separately for women and men.

Recommendations

To better understand gender issues and the best ways of addressing them in diverse contexts and across networks requires that the Bank learn from its own and others' experience through project design and implementation, research, and evaluations.

- *Recommendation 1: Gender concerns should be fully addressed in social assessments, in the selection of performance indicators, and in ICRs.*

Social assessments, performance indicators, and ICRs, as well as a systematic research program, should fully address gender concerns

- The social development family should include in its forthcoming guidelines on social assessment a discussion of how to link gender analysis, stakeholder analysis, and social assessments.

- Regional staff and management, with assistance from the Operations Policy Department (OPR), should ensure that the ongoing "retooling" of monitoring and evaluation indicators in the current portfolio (and especially in participation flagships and pilot projects) disaggregate data on men and women whenever appropriate.

- OPR should stipulate in the ICR guidelines (Operational Policy 13.55, currently being updated) that ICRs systematically check for and document results separately for men and women, when data are available, whether the project included some gender-related action or not.

- *Recommendation 2: The Office of the Senior Vice President and Chief Economist should advance the state of knowledge on gender issues by setting up a systematic program of research to examine the gender impact of project lending and policy reform.*

  - The research program should explicitly address both quantitative and qualitative dimensions of gender and should focus on both micro- and macro-level issues.

  - Such research requires routine collection of gender-disaggregated data, not only through projects but also through household survey instruments such as the Living Standard Measurement Surveys.

  - The research should be undertaken in consultation with all networks and OED.

Typically, gender issues are location-specific, and the regional gender action plans rightly call for systematic identification and prioritization of gender concerns during the CAS process, as stipulated in the current gender policy and in the CAS guidelines (Best Practice 2.11). But the action plans[2] may need to be adjusted in light of the more recent social development action plans and of the ongoing restructuring in some regions. Furthermore, the action plans do not set clear, time-bound implementation plans or mechanisms to monitor their implementation.

- *Recommendation 3: Each region should identify which elements of their gender action plans will be implemented within the next 36 months, establish time-bound, monitorable targets, and assign responsibility for monitoring implementation progress. The poverty reduction and economic management (PREM) network, working with the regions, should ensure that institution-wide progress is monitored.*

The ongoing changes in Bank structure and processes open a window of opportunity for faster progress in mainstreaming gender. But gender issues cut across all networks and their families, and they must be addressed through multisectoral and multidisciplinary work.

- *Recommendation 4: The network councils should ensure that each network and family takes steps to mainstream gender as appropriate in its work and, where possible, specify priority goals and targets. The proposed PREM gender family should make promoting synergistic interactions across the institution one of its priorities.*

Notes

1. At the time of the 1994 study, only 24 such projects were completed or were close to being completed.
2. Some regions merged their gender and their social development action plans; others kept them separated. Recommendation 3 applies in either case.

Resumen

Objetivos y métodos

En 1994, el Departamento de Evaluación de Operaciones (DEO) realizó un estudio interno (publicado en 1995; véase Murphy 1995) para determinar de qué manera quedó recogido el concepto de participación de la mujer en el proceso de desarrollo —y, posteriormente, el concepto más general de género— en las políticas y operaciones crediticias del Banco. Ese mismo año, el Banco publicó un documento de política —Política Operacional 4.20— y una nota sobre prácticas óptimas en que se recomienda que se integren a la labor del Banco las cuestiones relativas al género. Esta actualización del estudio de 1994 tiene dos objetivos: (1) confirmar o enmendar, sobre la base de un conjunto más completo de datos, las conclusiones preliminares formuladas en ese estudio, y (2) examinar las recientes operaciones crediticias y no crediticias para determinar si se ha avanzado en la aplicación de la política del Banco y de las recomendaciones formuladas por el DEO en 1994.

La actualización se basa en un examen independiente de la documentación disponible actualmente, incluidos documentos y archivos de proyectos, estudios económicos y sectoriales afines, y evaluaciones del DEO. Comprende un análisis de los resultados de 58 proyectos en los que se cumplieron actividades relativas al género, aprobados en el ejercicio de 1987 o con posterioridad y terminados antes del 30 de diciembre de 1995[1]. También se examina la incorporación de las cuestiones relativas a los sexos en los objetivos de 120 proyectos aprobados en los ejercicios de 1994 y 1995 y se analizan las características de todas las operaciones de financiamiento para fines de inversión aprobadas en los ejercicios de 1994, 1995 y 1996 en que se hayan propuesto actividades relativas al género —un total de 185 proyectos. Finalmente, del estudio se examina el tratamiento del tema del género en determinados estudios sectoriales. El personal del Banco contribuyó a través de consultas con grupos de interesados y entrevistas individuales. La administración del Banco puso a disposición del DEO un informe sobre la aplicación de las recomendaciones derivadas del estudio de 1994.

Principales conclusiones

La proporción de proyectos que incorporaban actividades relativas al género y que han logrado sus objetivos —es decir, cuyos resultados se estimaron satisfactorios— es relativamente mayor que el porcentaje de los proyectos que no incluyeron estas actividades, ejecutados en sectores similares y aprobados durante los mismos ejercicios (Capítulo 2).

De los 54 proyectos terminados aprobados durante el ejercicio de 1987 o con posterioridad en los sectores de agricultura y recursos humanos que incluyeron actividades relativas al género, el 74 por ciento dio resultados satisfactorios, mientras que de los 81 proyectos ejecutados en sectores similares, pero que no incluyeron esas actividades, sólo el 65 por ciento tuvo resultados satisfactorios.

Cuando las metas relativas al género se incorporan explícitamente a los objetivos principales del proyecto, las posibilidades de cumplir dichas metas son mayores (Capítulo 2).

Los análisis de regresión confirman la conclusión formulada en 1994 en el sentido de que los objetivos relativos al género se cumplen con mayor frecuencia si están sólidamente integrados en los objetivos centrales del proyecto, en lugar de formar parte de un componente independiente.

En comparación con los proyectos terminados que se habían aprobado entre los ejercicios de 1987 y 1991, la preparación de las actividades relativas al género mejoró considerablemente en los proyectos aprobados en los ejercicios de 1994 y 1995 (Capítulo 3).

Las dos terceras partes de los proyectos recientes con actividades relativas al género incluyeron análisis numerosos o de mayor nivel sobre este tema, en comparación con sólo el 16 por ciento de los proyectos terminados. En más del 70 por ciento de los proyectos recientes se han incorporado aspectos relativos al género en los objetivos generales, mientras que sólo aproximadamente la mitad de los proyectos terminados han incluido esos aspectos. Muchas veces, se realizaron simultáneamente análisis de enfoques participatorios y estudios de mejor nivel de la problemática del género.

No obstante, aún existen muchas posibilidades de aumentar la proporción de proyectos y estrategias de asistencia a países que abordan sistemáticamente las cuestiones relativas al género (capítulos 3 y 4, respectivamente).

En los últimos tres años, el porcentaje de proyectos que incluyeron actividades relativas al género se mantuvo en alrededor del 30 por ciento de la cartera de inversiones. Este porcentaje es inferior al máximo observado a comienzos de la década de 1990, época en que se estaba acercando al 45 por ciento-50 por ciento, y que probablemente es un tope realista. En el caso de las estrategias de asistencia a los países —según se estipula en la Política Operacional 4.20— el tratamiento del tema sigue siendo irregular, y en los informes finales de ejecución (IFE) dicha cobertura es escasa.

Conclusiones

Los resultados de la actualización demuestran que se está realizando una excelente labor y que el progreso alcanzado ha guardado relación con las recomendaciones formuladas por el DEO en 1994 (Capítulo 1). Las oficinas regionales han presentado interesantes propuestas y están finalizando la preparación de planes de acción para abordar la problemática del género. El alto nivel profesional y la dedicación de gran parte del personal —tanto de aquellos cuya labor está directamente relacionada con las cuestiones del género como de los jefes de proyecto— es ejemplar. La conclusión de que hay una vinculación entre la incorporación de las actividades relativas al género a los proyectos y el logro satisfactorio de los objetivos generales de éstos reafirma la actual política de incorporar la problemática del género a las operaciones del Banco. La administración superior y el Directorio Ejecutivo han adoptado una sólida posición de vanguardia en este terreno.

La actualización demuestra también que la labor relativa al género podría reforzar otras propuestas destinadas a convertir al desarrollo social en un elemento central del programa estratégico del Banco, además de beneficiarse de dichas propuestas. Estas iniciativas ofrecen grandes oportunidades para incorporar la problemática del género en la labor del Banco al vincular el análisis de esas cuestiones a las evaluaciones sociales, al incluir estos temas entre los factores que identifican a las partes interesadas relevantes, y cuando sea pertinente, al asegurar que los indicadores del desempeño miden los resultados por separado para las mujeres y los hombres.

Recomendaciones

Para comprender mejor las cuestiones relativas al género y determinar cual es la mejor forma de abordarlas en distintas situaciones y diferentes redes, el Banco debe aprovechar las enseñanzas adquiridas mediante su propia experiencia y la de otros en la formulación y ejecución de proyectos, la investigación y la evaluación

- *Recomendación 1: Las cuestiones relativas al género deben abordarse íntegramente en las evaluaciones sociales, en la selección de indicadores del desempeño y en los IFE.*

  - Los temas relacionados con el desarrollo social deben incluir en sus futuras directrices para las evaluaciones sociales una reseña sobre la forma de vincular el análisis de la problemática del género al análisis de las partes interesadas y a las evaluaciones sociales.

  - El personal y la administración de las oficinas regionales, con la ayuda del Departamento de Políticas de Operaciones, deben garantizar que, al "reorganizarse" las tareas de seguimiento y los indicadores de evaluación de la actual cartera (sobre todo en los proyectos experimentales y de punta en materia de participación), se desglosen los datos de hombres y mujeres cuando así corresponda.

  - El Departamento de Políticas de Operaciones debe estipular en las directrices para los IFE (Política Operacional 13.55, actualmente en actualización) que, cuando haya datos disponibles, se verifiquen y documenten separadamente los resultados relativos a los hombres de los relativos a la mujer, sea que el proyecto incluya o no actividades relacionadas con el género.

- *Recomendación 2: La Oficina del Primer Vicepresidente y Primer Economista debe promover el conocimiento de las cuestiones relativas al género mediante la puesta en marcha de un programa sistemático de investigación destinado a examinar los efectos de los préstamos para proyectos y la reforma de las políticas en las cuestiones relativas al género.*

  - El programa de investigación debe abordar explícitamente los aspectos cuantitativos y cualitativos de la problemática del género y centrarse tanto en los problemas microeconómicos como macroeconómicos.

  - Para respaldar estas investigaciones será necesario recopilar periódicamente información oportuna, desglosada por sexo, no sólo a través de los proyectos sino también mediante instrumentos que se usan en las encuestas de hogares, como el Estudio de medición de los niveles de vida.

- Esta investigaciones deben realizarse en consulta con las diferentes redes y el DEO.

Normalmente, las cuestiones relativas al género tienen un alcance estrictamente local, y en los planes de acción para abordar su problemática formulados por las oficinas regionales se propone, acertadamente, que en las estrategias de asistencia a los países esas cuestiones sean identificadas sistemáticamente y organizadas de acuerdo a un orden de prioridad, como se estipula en la correspondiente política actual y en las directrices sobre las estrategias de asistencia a los países (Práctica Óptima 2.11). Sin embargo, podría ser necesario ajustar los planes de acción en vista de la formulación, más recientemente, de los planes de acción para el desarrollo social[2] y de la reestructuración que se está realizando en algunas oficinas regionales. Además, los planes de acción no incluyen mecanismos ni programas de ejecución definidos con fechas fijas para supervisar su puesta en marcha.

- *Recomendación 3: Las oficinas regionales deben decidir, en el curso de los próximos 36 meses, qué aspectos de sus planes de acción sobre la problemática del género serán puestos en práctica, establecer objetivos a plazo fijo que puedan supervisarse, y seleccionar a los responsables de seguir el progreso de la ejecución. La red sobre Reducción de la Pobreza y Gestión Económica, en colaboración con las oficinas regionales, debe velar por que se realice un seguimiento del proceso de ejecución a nivel institucional.*

Los actuales cambios en la estructura y en los procedimientos del Banco ofrecen una oportunidad para acelerar la incorporación de las cuestiones del género en las actividades de la institución. No obstante, estos problemas trascienden la labor de las redes y sus temas y deben abordarse mediante una labor multisectorial y multidisciplinaria.

- *Recomendación 4: Los consejos de las redes deben velar por que en cada red y en cada tema se adopten, cuando sea necesario, medidas destinadas a incorporar las cuestiones relativas al género en sus actividades y por que se fijen objetivos prioritarios específicos cuando sea posible. El tema propuesto del género en la red sobre Reducción de la Pobreza y Gestión Económica debe dar prioridad al fomento de la interacción sinérgica entre las diferentes entidades de la institución.*

Notas

1. En la fecha en que se realizó el estudio de 1994, sólo 24 proyectos se habían terminado o estaban próximos a terminarse.
2. Algunas oficinas regionales fusionaron sus planes de acción sobre cuestiones del género con el de desarrollo social, mientras que otras los mantuvieron separados. La recomendación 3 se aplica en ambos casos.

Résumé

Objectifs et méthodes

En 1994, une étude effectuée par le Département de l'évaluation des opérations (DEO) (publiée plus tard; voir Murphy 1995) a montré comment la notion de rôle des femmes dans le développement et, par la suite, celle plus large de parité entre les sexes, en sont arrivées à être incorporées aux politiques et aux opérations de prêt de la Banque. La même année, la Banque a publié un document de politique générale, la Directive opérationnelle 4.20, et une note sur les pratiques optimales qui préconisent l'intégration de la parité des sexes aux activités de la Banque. Cette mise à jour de l'étude de 1994 a un double objectif : (1) valider ou réviser les constatations préliminaires de l'étude de 1994 sur la base d'un ensemble de données d'expérience plus vaste; et (2) examiner les opérations récentes, de prêt et autres, afin de déterminer si des progrès ont été accomplis dans la mise en oeuvre de la politique de la Banque et des recommandations formulées par le DEO en 1994.

La mise à jour est fondée sur les conclusions d'une analyse indépendante de la documentation existante, y compris les dossiers de projets, les études économiques et sectorielles afférentes, et les évaluations du DEO. Elle analyse les résultats de 58 projets approuvés à compter de l'exercice 87 et clos le 30 décembre 1995 au plus tard[1]. Elle examine aussi la place de la parité des sexes dans les objectifs de 120 projets approuvés pendant les exercices 94 et 95 et analyse les caractéristiques de tous les prêts d'investissement comprenant explicitement des mesures dans ce domaine et qui ont été approuvés pendant les exercices 94, 95 et 96 — 185 projets au total. Enfin, elle examine la place de la parité des sexes dans un certain nombre d'études sectorielles. Les services de la Banque ont participé à l'étude dans le cadre de groupes de discussion et d'entretiens individuels. La direction de la Banque a transmis au DEO un rapport sur l'exécution de la liste de recommandations figurant dans l'étude de 1994.

Principales constatations

Les projets comportant des mesures relatives à la parité des sexes ont atteint leurs objectifs généraux — c'est-à-dire ont reçu la mention « résultats satisfaisants » — dans une proportion plus importante que les projets qui concernaient des secteurs analogues approuvés au cours des mêmes exercices mais ne comportaient pas de mesures relatives à la parité des sexes (Chapitre 2).

Soixante-quatorze pour cent des 54 projets achevés dans les secteurs de l'agriculture ou des ressources humaines, qui comprenaient des mesures relatives à la parité des sexes et qui avaient été approuvés pendant ou après l'exercice 87, ont été classés comme globalement satisfaisants, contre 65 pour cent dans le cas des 81 projets dont la répartition sectorielle était analogue mais qui ne comportaient pas de mesures relatives à la parité des sexes.

Les projets dont les objectifs principaux comprennent expressément des objectifs de parité sont ceux qui ont le plus de chances de les atteindre (Chapitre 2).

L'analyse de régression confirme les constatations faites en 1994, à savoir que les objectifs de parité ont plus de chances de se réaliser s'ils sont bien intégrés aux grands objectifs des projets au lieu de constituer un volet à part.

La qualité des mesures relatives à la parité des sexes s'est sensiblement améliorée pour les projets approuvés durant les exercices 94 et 95 par rapport aux projets approuvés entre les exercices 87 et 91 (Chapitre 3).

Les deux tiers des projets récents qui comportent des interventions dans ce domaine contiennent des analyses relativement approfondies des questions de parité des sexes, contre 16 pour cent seulement dans les projets terminés. Les considérations de parité des sexes étaient intégrées aux objectifs généraux dans plus de 70 pour cent des projets récents, contre la moitié environ dans le cas des projets terminés. Il est fréquent qu'une meilleure qualité d'analyse des questions de parité des sexes coexiste avec une approche concertée.

Mais le nombre de projets et de stratégies d'aide-pays (SAP) qui prennent systématiquement en compte les questions de parité des sexes pourrait être sensiblement plus élevé (chapitres 3 et 4 respectivement).

La proportion des projets comportant des mesures relatives à la parité des sexes tourne autour de 30 pour cent du portefeuille d'investissements depuis trois ans, soit une baisse par rapport au pic du début des années 90, où elle avait approché les 45–50 pour cent (ce qui constitue peut-être une limite supérieure réaliste). Les SAP abordent cette question, conformément à la Directive opérationnelle 4.20, mais de manière inégale. Les rapports de fin d'exécution (RFE) n'en font état que sporadiquement.

Conclusions

Il ressort de cette mise à jour qu'un excellent travail est accompli et que l'évolution est conforme aux recommandations formulées par le DEO en 1994 (Chapitre 1). Les bureaux régionaux ont pris des initiatives intéressantes et l'on termine des plans d'action relatifs à la parité des sexes. La qualité et le dévouement de beaucoup d'agents de la Banque, qu'ils soient spécialisés dans ce domaine ou qu'ils s'agisse des chefs de projets en général, sont exemplaires. Le fait qu'on ait constaté une corrélation positive entre les mesures relatives à la parité des sexes contenues dans les projets et la réalisation satisfaisante de leurs objectifs généraux est un argument en faveur de la politique actuelle, qui consiste à intégrer la parité des sexes aux opérations courantes de la Banque. La Direction et le Conseil ont clairement fixé les orientations dans ce domaine.

La mise à jour indique également que les activités concernant la parité des sexes peuvent renforcer d'autres initiatives qui ont pour but de faire du développement social un élément clé de la stratégie de la Banque — et qu'elles peuvent en être elles-mêmes renforcées. Ces initiatives fournissent d'excellentes occasions d'incorporer les activités relatives à la parité des sexes aux travaux de la Banque, en liant l'analyse de la problématique hommes-femmes aux évaluations sociales, en plaçant le sexe parmi les facteurs qui identifient les parties prenantes pertinentes et, lorsque cela est utile, en faisant en sorte que les indicateurs de performance mesurent séparément les résultats concernant les femmes et les résultats concernant les hommes.

Recommandations

Pour mieux comprendre la problématique hommes-femmes et les meilleurs moyens de s'attaquer aux problèmes dans ce domaine, dans des contextes divers et dans l'ensemble des services administratifs, il est impératif que la Banque tire les enseignements de son expérience et de celle des autres dans les domaines de la conception et de l'exécution des projets, de la recherche, et des évaluations.

- *Première recommandation : Il faut que les évaluations sociales, la sélection des indicateurs de performance et les RFE prennent pleinement en compte les questions de parité des sexes.*

  - Le groupe du développement social devrait incorporer aux directives sur les évaluations sociales qu'il doit publier prochainement une discussion des moyens de lier l'analyse de la problématique hommes-femmes, l'analyse des parties prenantes et les évaluations sociales.

  - Il serait bon que les services et les cadres régionaux, avec le concours du Département de la politique opérationnelle (OPR), veillent à ce que les révisions en cours des indicateurs de suivi et d'évaluation du portefeuille actuel (en particulier dans le cas des projets participatifs modèles ou des projets pilotes) prennent soin de séparer les données concernant les hommes et les femmes lorsque cela est approprié.

  - Il conviendrait qu'OPR stipule, dans les directives concernant la préparation des RFE (Directive de politique opérationnelle 13.55, en cours de révision), que les RFE doivent vérifier et décrire systématiquement les résultats pour les hommes et pour les femmes de manière séparée, lorsque les données sont disponibles, que le projet comporte ou non des interventions dans le domaine de la parité des sexes.

- *Deuxième recommandation : Il faudrait que le Bureau du Premier Vice-président et économiste en chef fasse progresser les connaissances sur les questions de parité des sexes en établissant un programme de recherche systématique, qui examine l'impact des prêts et des programmes de réformes sur la parité des sexes.*

  - Le programme de recherche devrait considérer à la fois les dimensions quantitatives et qualitatives de la problématique hommes-femmes et porter aussi bien sur les aspects macroéconomiques que microéconomiques.

  - Pour alimenter les activités de recherche, il faudra que des données appropriées soient réunies systématiquement, par sexe, non seulement dans le cadre des projets, mais également par le biais d'enquêtes sur les ménages telles que les Enquêtes sur la mesure des niveaux de vie.

- Il serait bon que ces recherches soient menées en consultation avec tous les réseaux administratifs et le DEO.

En général, les questions de parité des sexes sont circonscrites sur le plan géographique et c'est à juste titre que les plans d'action régionaux pour la parité des sexes précisent qu'il convient dans tous les cas d'identifier systématiquement les problèmes et de les classer par rang de priorité pendant le préparation du SAP, comme le stipulent les directives en vigueur concernant la parité des sexes (Best Practice 2.11). Mais il peut être nécessaire de modifier les plans d'action[2] compte tenu de ceux qui ont été adoptés plus récemment dans le domaine du développement social et des restructurations en cours dans certaines régions. De plus, les plans d'action ne fixent pas de systèmes d'exécution clairs, assortis de dates précises, ou de mécanismes pour en suivre l'exécution.

- *Troisième recommandation : Chaque région devrait identifier les éléments de son plan d'action relatif à la parité des sexes qui seront appliqués dans les 36 prochains mois, fixer des objectifs temporels fixes et vérifiables et désigner les responsables du suivi de l'exécution. Il appartiendra au réseau Réduction de la pauvreté et gestion économique (PREM) de s'assurer, en coopération avec les régions, que l'on suit les progrès accomplis à l'échelle de l'institution.*

Les changements en cours dans les structures et les méthodes de travail de la Banque offrent une occasion unique d'accélérer l'intégration des questions de parité des sexes aux opérations. Mais ces questions se posent au niveau de tous les réseaux et de tous les groupes, et il faut s'y attaquer selon une stratégie multisectorielle et pluridisciplinaire.

- *Quatrième recommandation : Les conseils de réseaux devraient veiller à ce que chaque réseau et chaque groupe agisse pour intégrer la parité des sexes à ses activités, selon les besoins, et, partout où cela est possible, précise ses buts et objectifs prioritaires. Le groupe de la parité des sexes envisagé à PREM devrait se fixer comme priorité, entre autres, de promouvoir la synergie des activités menées dans l'ensemble de l'institution.*

Notes

1. Au moment où l'étude de 1994 a été réalisée, seuls 24 projets de ce type avaient été terminés ou tiraient à leur fin.
2. Certaines régions ont combiné leurs plans d'action concernant la parité des sexes et leurs plans d'action pour le développement social, tandis que d'autres ont conservé des plans distincts. La troisième recommandation qui est applicable dans les deux cas.

1. Introduction

The Bank position on gender

The Fourth International Conference on Women, which took place in Beijing in September 1995, was the largest conference ever held solely on the subject of women. Sponsored by the United Nations (UN), the Beijing conference, as it came to be known, prompted participating governments and agencies to take stock of past experience and, like the previous UN-sponsored conferences on women, encouraged agencies such as the World Bank to do more about gender.[1]

Bank staff contributed to the many regional and topical preparatory meetings that preceded the conference. Bank research and policy were distilled in several documents presented at the conference, most notably *Advancing Gender Equality: From Concept to Action* (World Bank 1995a) and *Toward Gender Equality: The Role of Public Policy* (World Bank 1995e). The Bank's delegation was led, for the first time, by the President.

Following the conference, internal seminars such as the two-week Beyond Beijing program gave added visibility to the issue of gender within the Bank. Senior management asked the regional offices to prepare comprehensive action plans, a task now close to completion; a committee on gender was established to report periodically to the President; closer Bank relations were developed with nongovernmental organizations (NGOs); and outside experts were invited to participate in a consultative group on gender that would advise Bank management.

The Beijing conference and the events associated with it took place just 18 months after the Bank issued its internal policy paper, together with an Operational Directive (O.D. 4.20) and a Best Practice Note which provide guidance to staff. The policy paper asserted that the Bank was committed to mainstreaming gender concerns into its operations and thus provided the legitimacy and official support that had been lacking. The Bank strategy for implementing its gender policy is based on four principles, summarized in Box 1.1.

The Bank's strategy for implementing its gender policy is based on mainstreaming, focus on selected sectors and countries, and integration in country programming

Since 1994, the Bank has also taken steps to promote more participatory approaches to development and to better integrate the social dimensions of development into Bank lending and nonlending services. Participation action plans have been under implementation since July 1995 in each region and central vice presidency. More recently, a task force on social development reported to Bank management that social factors are an integral part of the development paradigm and that they must be incorporated in Bank analytical and lending work. In this context, addressing gender concerns is relevant for promoting participatory approaches, better identifying stakeholders, and better integrating social factors into Bank work. Current efforts on participation and social development should open additional opportunities for addressing gender issues.

BOX 1.1: BASIC PRINCIPLES OF BANK STRATEGY ON GENDER, APRIL 1994

The policy paper establishes the rationale for the Bank's involvement in gender issues on the basis of improved efficiency, poverty alleviation, and equity. Noting that gender is a culturally sensitive issue, the paper emphasizes the borrower's autonomy in identifying priorities and selecting strategies. It provides an excellent summary of the payoffs and barriers to integrating both men and women into the development process. The Bank strategy, as discussed in the policy paper and specified in the Operational Directive, is based on the following four principles:

- *Mainstreaming.* The policy paper formalizes the Bank's commitment to analyzing the likely effects of proposed actions on women and men in all analytical and project work (as appropriate) rather than addressing issues that affect women through women-only projects.

- *Sectoral focus.* The paper argues that the Bank should concentrate its efforts on expanding girls' education, improving women's health, increasing women's participation in the labor force, expanding women's options in agriculture, and providing financial services to women.

- *Country focus.* The paper proposes that the Bank focus its efforts on countries with the greatest gap between men and women.

- *Country strategy.* The paper calls for particular attention to gender issues in economic and sector work, beginning with poverty assessments, and mandates that plans for dealing with gender issues be included in country assistance strategy papers.

The 1994 OED study: findings and recommendations

A 1994 OED study (later published; see Murphy 1995) traced how the concepts of women in development (WID) and gender-related activities have evolved within the Bank and how Bank policies and lending reflected these concepts.[2]

Four factors were associated with successful implementation of projects with gender-related actions...

The study found that, for projects with some type of gender-related action specified in their project documents, the following factors were associated with successful implementation but were not present in unsuccessful cases: (1) country involvement with and commitment to both gender-related actions and the project as a whole; (2) gender analysis (an examination of the roles, activities, and constraints specific to men and women and pertinent to project concerns), followed by clear integration of gender-related considerations into overall project objectives; (3) input from staff experienced in addressing gender issues; and (4) attention to gender-related interventions during supervision. Overall outcomes (satisfactory or unsatisfactory ratings) for projects with and without gender-related activities did not differ across sectors. These findings were preliminary, since only 196 of the 615 projects with gender-related actions had been evaluated at that time, including only a handful of projects designed during the late 1980s.

Table 1.1 reproduces the ledger of recommendations presented in the 1994 OED study, together with the response made by Bank management when the Joint Audit Committee reviewed the study in August 1994.[3]

Management reported on the Bank's progress in implementing the recommendations in July 1995. In preparation for a briefing to the Committee on

Development Effectiveness (CODE), the Poverty and Social Policy Department, in consultation with the regions, drafted an update of progress in May 1996. A review of material cited in these reports shows that, in general, the activities mandated in the management response have been implemented as planned. Some examples are given below. Chapters 3 and 4 provide more substantive analyses of gender in recent project and economic and sector work (ESW), respectively.

...country involvement and commitment, gender analysis and integration in project goals, input from experienced staff, and attention to gender issues during supervision

Management report on recommendation 1:
including staff with gender experience in ESW and project work

Gender expertise was defined in the study as "having experience with integrating gender aspects in sector and lending work." Such expertise does not necessarily require formal training or experience specifically in gender work. A recent OED experience confirms that a high level of gender expertise can be found among task managers who have never worked as gender specialists. OED selected 85 task managers for focus group interviews (described in Chapter 5) on the basis of excellent integration of gender issues in the work they have done in the last three years. Only three of the invitees were currently assigned to gender specialist positions, and two more had worked on such positions in the past. Yet all of the task managers had shown an excellent grasp of gender issues in their work.

Management reported that gender expertise was applied to a variety of tasks. For example, gender specialists participated in the supervision of the General Education Project (Cr. 2118), the Female Secondary Assistance Project (Cr. 2469), and the Health Project (Cr. 2259) in Bangladesh. This experience is noteworthy because both the 1994 study and this update (Chapter 2) conclude that attention to planned gender-related actions often decreases during supervision. Similarly, the involvement of gender specialists led to clear recognition of gender concerns in those sectors where traditionally it has received little attention. The recent poverty assessment for Togo (World Bank 1996b) is an example of effective cooperation between a task manager with a strong awareness of gender issues and a gender specialist working as a peer reviewer. The document systematically identifies the gender dimensions of poverty: the vulnerability of women and girls; the pressure of cultural norms and traditions; and the inequalities in access to education, health, and production factors such as land.

Management report on recommendation 2:
formal discussions of gender-related actions with the borrowers

The management update refers to country-level workshops, country implementation reviews, and in some cases meetings of development agency consortia. Such meetings have been used to help member countries better understand and support gender-related actions, especially in Asia. In countries such as Chile and El Salvador, the Bank has supported the establishment or strengthening of government institutions dealing with gender issues. These institutions help to create a permanent forum for discussing gender issues with the government. Gender issues have been discussed at meetings linked to the Special Program for Africa, especially the integration of gender and poverty issues in adjustment lending operations. Although not discussed in the management response, the Bank's increased interaction with NGOs on gender-related issues may also help promote borrower attention to these issues.

Another approach to promoting a dialogue on gender issues with borrowers has been through regional or country-level seminars that promote discussion

Table 1.1: OED ledger—gender issues in Bank lending: an overview

Major OED recommendations	*Management response*
Country departments and gender staff in central vice presidencies and the regions should look for opportunities to use the following steps—and test others—whenever gender issues are relevant.	
1. To integrate gender issues into economic and sector work (ESW) and the portfolio, task managers should ensure that staff or consultants with gender experience are included in working groups during sector work, project preparation and appraisal, thematic supervisions, reviews of the portfolio, or assessments of gender issues at country level, as appropriate.	Agreed. Gender issues are likely to be increasingly addressed in ESW and the portfolio as staff become more convinced of the importance of the issues and knowledge is disseminated through training tool kits. There are a variety of ways to integrate gender issues into ESW and the portfolio implemented by the regions and the central vice presidencies, including the use of gender specialists. Some regions (Asia, Africa) have systematically reviewed Initial Executive Project Summary, and the Technical Department gender teams are available to carry out follow up support where intervention would have the greatest impact. Europe and Central Asia (ECA) and Middle East and North Africa (MENA) regional offices have used their central pool women in development (WID) funds to help the integration process. Human Resources Development and Operations Policy Vice Presidency (HRO) also provides the support at all stages to selective country departments.
2. To increase member countries' understanding and support, country departments should formally discuss gender-related actions with the borrowers during country implementation reviews, in special workshops, or in meetings of the consortia of development agencies.	Agreed. Africa has adopted this consultative approach in the context of specific ESW or lending operations. Gender issues and economic adjustment will be a regular item for discussion at biannual Special Program for Africa fora. In ECA, a plan for dissemination is now a requirement for activities supported under the ECA WID Fund. MENA also plans to discuss gender issues at a future meeting of the Council of Advisers and at a regional seminar for high-level country officials. Asia and Latin America and the Caribbean regional office have also been discussing gender-related ESW with concerned borrowers and disseminating the outputs to a wider audience.

Major OED recommendations	*Management response*
3. When planning the preparation of a country assistance strategy paper, country departments should determine what steps, if any, are needed to ensure that the required statement on gender reflects a good understanding of the situation and contributes to the policy discussion with member countries.	Agreed. This is a strategic point of intervention which provides the opportunity for the identification of priorities and the allocation of human and financial resources to be deployed on incorporating the gender perspective into ESW and lending operations where it is relevant to the overall country assistance strategy (CAS). HRO is reviewing all CASs to ensure that the focus on priorities for gender is reflected. HRO plans to work with three selective country departments in FY95 to mainstream gender issues into the country strategy and the policy discussion with member countries. The Asia gender team plans to work with at least two country departments in FY95 to assist them in determining whether and how gender issues may be appropriately incorporated in the CAS and resultant ESW and lending program. A pilot program was established by the gender team in Africa to conduct systematic gender analysis of the household surveys and to provide models of the gender analysis of poverty assessments and hence eventually for the CAS.
4. To monitor implementation and facilitate evaluation of outcomes, member countries and sectoral divisions should select indicators with separate targets for men and women (or boys and girls) when appropriate, and plan data collection accordingly.	Agreed. Africa has adopted a system to monitor a clear specification of gender-related objectives or sex-specific objectives at all stages of the project cycle and quantitative specification of indicators for monitorable outcomes in staff appraisal reports and supervision reports.
5. Innovations to increase the participation of women in development planning and actions, or to better integrate gender issues in social assessments, should be promoted under the Fund for Innovative Approaches in Human and Social Development (FIAHS).	FIAHS should be used strictly for innovations. With respect to gender, such innovation would primarily include efforts to include gender issues in social assessments and to increase participation of women in development planning and decisionmaking. Management will take these considerations into account when approving the applications for the fund.

of research findings and their operational implications. For example, the Bank organized a regional seminar on gender and transition in Bucharest in February 1995. Papers on gender issues ranging from property rights and agrarian reform to gender dimensions in pension reform and the labor market and restructuring childcare were discussed with representatives and researchers from ten countries in Eastern Europe. These documents were used in subsequent sector work in several countries. At the country level, a seminar with officials from the Bangladesh Institute of Development Studies helped the borrower and the Bank better understand how providing access to credit through targeted programs enables poor women to increase family incomes. A workshop on participatory poverty monitoring and analysis, held in South Africa, brought key stakeholders together to agree on measures to monitor poverty, with special attention to the needs of women.

Management report on recommendation 3:
background work on gender issues for country assistance strategies (CASs)

The regional offices cite examples of good attention to gender in CASs. For example, the Nepal country assistance strategy identifies sectoral strategies that support improvements in the status of women in the country. In addition, the CAS recognizes that future lending operations in the country will benefit from the analytical work done in the context of the FY97 poverty assessment, itself based on gender-specific data collected by the Nepal Living Standards Survey. But management reports that only half of the CASs prepared during FY94–95 specifically addressed gender issues. Incorporating these issues in all CASs is a key focus of the regional gender action plans.

Management report on recommendation 4:
selecting gender-specific targets for key indicators when appropriate

Regional offices generally apply this recommendation in all project documents that clearly identify indicators. But the Africa program to monitor gender objectives at all phases of the project cycle (described in the original response) has been discontinued. Opportunities to improve data collection are not yet used systematically. This is reflected, for example, in the scarcity of information in supervision reports, midterm reviews, and implementation completion reports (ICRs) on how project activities may affect men and women differently.

Management report on recommendation 5:
support from the Fund for Innovative Approaches in Human and Social Development (FIAHS) for work on gender issues

Management had agreed to take gender into consideration when reviewing proposals for funding by FIAHS. It reports on the use of FIAHS funding in projects such as the Armenia Social Investment Fund (Cr. 2784), where FIAHS covered the costs of a consultant who ensured that the microenterprise component would allow for the participation of local groups, including women's groups. In Nicaragua the fund supported a social assessment of a project's likely impacts on women in terms of better access to water services and improved health and nutrition status.

Reports from FIAHS managers mention projects not listed in the management report. For example, the Egypt Matruh Resource Management Project (Cr. 2504) used FIAHS funding to conduct beneficiary assessments with women's groups to reassess the groups' priorities with regard to their participation in the project.

Objectives of this update

After reviewing the 1994 study, the Board's Joint Audit Committee (now CODE) commented that until gender issues are mainstreamed into overall Bank activities, the Bank's development objectives will not be achieved. The committee and Bank management asked OED to update the study as more evaluations of projects with gender-related actions became available and as it became possible to identify the initial effects of the policy paper and the OED recommendations.

This update has two objectives: (1) to confirm or revise the 1994 study's preliminary findings on the basis of a larger body of evidence and (2) to identify changes in the prevalence and quality of recent gender-related analyses and lending in light of the policy paper and the OED recommendations. The update incorporates evidence from a total of 802 projects with gender-related actions approved between FY67 and FY96. It reviews the results of 58 of these projects (approved in FY87–91) for which outcomes have been evaluated in order to verify the findings of the 1994 study (Chapter 2). The study analyzes the overall quality of lending in FY94–95 for gender integration and compares it with completed projects (Chapter 3), and reviews recent ESW and country assistance strategies (Chapter 4). Together, chapters 3 and 4 provide a first assessment of how the four strategic principles identified in the Bank gender policy are being implemented. Specifically, Chapter 3 discusses the sectoral distribution and overall mainstreaming of gender in the portfolio, while Chapter 4 reviews whether Bank efforts are concentrated in countries with the greatest needs and whether gender issues are addressed in the CASs. The last chapter summarizes recent institutional changes and presents the views of task managers and gender specialists on what mainstreaming gender should mean in the context of Bank work and on the actions that are needed to accelerate progress.

The update draws from four sources: (1) project documents, project files, related ESW, and publications; (2) OED audits, impact evaluations, and ratings of completed projects; (3) material prepared by the regional offices and the central gender analysis and policy team (GAP), including progress reports to the Board, reviews of progress on the OED 1994 recommendations, and draft action plans; and (4) extensive individual and focus group interviews with staff in the Bank and at other agencies.

Notes

1. Conferences in 1975, 1980, and 1985 held in Mexico, Copenhagen, and Nairobi, respectively (Murphy 1995).
2. The report defined the difference between women in development (WID) and gender as follows: "The...term [WID] was applied to actions designed to ensure that women benefited, or at least did not suffer, from development efforts. Gender-related development activities, on the other hand, take a broader view of the differences in behavior expected of women and of men, seeking their causes and their consequences for economic and human resources development. Gender-related actions can prevent deleterious consequences and maximize the potential contributions specific to women or men through direct intervention on immediate constraints, or through strategic changes in the legal and regulatory framework of the country" (Murphy 1995, 23).
3. All Operations Evaluation Department studies contain a ledger of key recommendations prepared when the study is being finalized. The ledger includes the management response to the recommendations and the steps proposed to implement them. Bank management updates the ledger annually, comparing actual implementation with the proposed plan.

2. Outcomes and implementation experience for completed projects

The 1994 findings described in Box 2.1 were preliminary, since only a handful of projects designed during the late 1980s had been evaluated at the time of the study. This chapter discusses the outcome and implementation experience for the 58 projects with gender-related action approved in FY87 or later and completed by December 1995, for which a project completion report (PCR) or ICR could be obtained.[1] This chapter reports on factors associated with successful implementation of the gender objectives among the 58 completed projects, together with quantitative analyses to measure the gender contribution to positive outcomes. Finally, it assesses the quality of the completion reports with respect to gender.

Table 2.1 shows that the sectoral distribution of these 58 completed projects is in line with the areas—mainly agriculture and human resources—selected for attention to women in FY87. While these projects, by definition, included some gender-related action, the gender objectives were often modest. Some simply mentioned that women and girls would also benefit from the project—for example, the Malawi Education Sector Project (Cr. 1767), which set targets for the number of girls attending secondary schools financed by the project. About a third developed more elaborate gender objectives for improving women's productive efficiency or for improving welfare of women and children. Strategies to meet productivity objectives included providing extension services for women farmers (Benin Second Borgou Rural Development Project, Cr. 1877); vocational training for women reentering the work force (Mexico Manpower Project, Ln. 2876); and improving the availability of water, thus freeing women's time for productive activities (Albania Rural Poverty Alleviation Pilot, Cr. 2461). Strategies expected to meet welfare objectives included providing maternal and child care programs (Oman Health Project, Ln. 2807) and improving the nutritional status of pregnant and lactating women.

Projects with gender-related action were more likely to reach a satisfactory outcome than those without—and were more likely to be rated as sustainable

Outcomes for projects with gender objectives

Historically, the proportion of projects rated as satisfactory varies across sectors and regions. Table 2.2 gives outcome, sustainability, and institutional development ratings for the 54 projects in the agriculture and human resources sectors that had gender-related action and compares them with those of projects in the same sectors and within the same approval period. Projects with gender-related action were more likely to reach a satisfactory outcome than projects without such actions—74 percent against 65 percent—and they were more likely to be rated as sustainable—54 percent against 46 percent. The difference in achieving a substantial level of institutional development is also great—43 percent against 32 percent. But overall, institutional development was lower in projects with gender-related action.

Box 2.1: The 1994 findings on design features associated with successful implementation

The Operations Evaluation Department study found that, for projects with some specified gender-related action, the following factors were associated with successful implementation but were not present in unsuccessful cases: (1) borrower involvement with and commitment to both gender-related actions and the project as a whole; (2) analysis of the roles, activities, and constraints specific to men and women and pertinent to project concerns (gender analysis), followed by clear integration of gender-related objectives with overall project objectives; (3) inputs from staff experienced in addressing gender issues; and (4) attention to gender-related interventions during supervision. Overall outcomes (satisfactory or unsatisfactory ratings) for projects with and without gender-related activities did not differ.

But such projects may also reflect better identification of the target population, design, and implementation

The 54 completed projects discussed above were designed in or after FY87, at a time when the level of attention to gender increased significantly. Looking back further to projects approved since FY67, the difference in outcomes between completed projects with and without gender-related action almost disappears. Of the projects approved since FY67 and for which ratings are available, 69 percent of the 262 with gender-related action were rated satisfactory, while 71 percent of all projects in the same years and the same sectors were considered satisfactory.[2]

Of course, the presence of some gender-related action in a project may reflect better identification of target populations or generally better design. Also, well-implemented projects were the most likely to achieve their gender objectives: all the projects in this sample that successfully met their gender objectives received satisfactory ratings for overall project outcome. On the other hand, a satisfactory rating for project outcomes does not necessarily mean that the gender objectives were achieved. Only 27 of the 58 completed projects across all sectors achieved their gender objectives (7 projects were canceled early on or were severely disrupted by civil wars). For all regions except Africa, 47 percent of projects with satisfactory outcomes also achieved their intended gender-related actions. In Africa, only 24 percent did so. This difference could well be a temporary situation linked to the generally lower rating for institutional development in that region, and to the fact that the Africa regional office began to incorporate gender-related actions in its projects ahead of the other regions (see Box 2.2). At this time, the number of completed projects is still too small for a more detailed analysis of possible differences across regions.

Implementation experience

The implementation experience and levels of achievement in the 58 completed projects highlight several factors associated with successful cases but not present in unsuccessful projects.[3] It also highlights weak areas in design, supervision, and evaluation.

Project design in the late 1980s was rarely based on solid gender analysis

Men and women everywhere usually have different responsibilities, undertaken with various degrees of flexibility and different priorities. If the labor demand, timing, or priority of one task changes, either the restructured task

TABLE 2.1: DISTRIBUTION OF THE 58 COMPLETED PROJECTS ACROSS SECTORS, BY YEAR OF APPROVAL

OED sector	*FY87*	*FY88*	*FY89*	*FY90*	*FY91*	*FY92*	*FY93*	*Total*
Agriculture	8	3	5	5	3	3	1	28
Human resources[a]	8	6	4	4	3	1	—	26
Finance	—	—	1	—	1	—	—	2
Water supply and sanitation	—	—	1	—	—	—	—	1
Urban	—	—	—	1	—	—	—	1
Total	16	9	11	10	7	4	1	58

— Not applicable.
a. The human resources sector includes four social investment fund projects, which were reclassified in FY94 under a new category of "social sector" in the Bank's management information system.
Source: World Bank management information system.

TABLE 2.2: A COMPARISON OF OUTCOMES FOR PROJECTS WITH AND WITHOUT GENDER-RELATED ACTION, APPROVED FY87-93, AGRICULTURE AND HUMAN RESOURCES SECTORS *(percent)*

	With gender-related action N = 54	*Without gender-related action, same years and sectors* N = 81
Outcome		
Satisfactory	74	65
Sustainability		
Likely	54	46
Institutional development		
Substantial	43	32
Modest	17	42

Source: OED.

Gender analysis identifies project opportunities and risks by ascertaining the roles and responsibilities of men and women and potential areas of conflict

must not conflict with other tasks or all the tasks must be modified. Effective project design must include a review of both men's and women's roles and responsibilities that is detailed enough to identify potential conflicts and strategies to resolve them. Gender analysis establishes what these various responsibilities are and the demands they generate throughout the year in order to identify opportunities and risks. The project staff appraisal reports (SARs) provide evidence that an adequate gender analysis was done for only 16 percent of the 58 projects. Even then, it was rarely reflected in project design. Only 9 of the 58 projects had a high or substantial level of gender analysis that included a description of roles, tasks, and responsibilities for various categories of men and women and a discussion of how these would be changed by the project.[4]

Gender objectives that were well integrated in project objectives were more likely to be implemented

Of the 51 projects fully implemented, those in which gender objectives were fully integrated into the main objectives were more likely to achieve their gender goals. For example, the social fund projects (Cr. 2212 and Cr. 2401) in Honduras helped finance subprojects to meet the basic needs of the population. Care was taken to promote the types of subprojects, such as small-scale

Box 2.2: Logit analysis of completed projects[a]

Unconditional logistic regression analyses were carried out for the 58 completed projects for which ratings were available. Univariate analyses resulted in the following findings:

- All projects rated high for achievement of gender objectives by the Operations Evaluation Department also received satisfactory ratings for achievement of general objectives.

- Projects rated as likely to be sustainable were also more likely to achieve their gender objectives.

- Projects approved in more recent years were more likely to achieve their gender objectives, perhaps in part because they were less likely to have been extended—often a sign of implementation difficulties—and because many of the newer projects were concentrated in the human resources sectors.

Two weaker relationships were observed:

- So far, gender objectives were achieved less often in Africa than in the other regions (see section on outcomes for projects with gender objectives for a cautionary discussion of this observation).

- Gender objectives were achieved most often for human resources projects.

The multivariate analyses, while controlling for intercept, fiscal year of approval, source of funding, commitment amount, and the income level of the country, found four factors that contributed to the achievement of gender objectives. Three were positive and very significant—integration of gender objectives into the overall project objectives, institutional development impact, and the likelihood of sustainability. A human resources sector dummy and an Africa region dummy were both found to be positive and mildly significant.

It is important to note that the logit analysis indicates an association between achievement of gender objectives and these variables; it does not necessarily imply a causal relationship.

a. See annex for a more detailed description of the methodology.

farms and family gardens, that would benefit women heads of household. Also, to encourage women to bring in their children for preventive care, food coupons were distributed through the health centers. These efforts to reach women through the main project components rather than a separate "women" program were successful. Fifty-one percent of the projects with well integrated gender objectives did achieve them, well above the 29 percent achievement rate for all 51 fully implemented projects. A logit analysis confirmed that integration of gender objectives into project objectives contributes significantly to the achievement of the gender objectives (Box 2.2).

Efforts to reach women through the main project components rather than separate "women" programs succeeded

Gender issues were not systematically reviewed during supervision

The 1994 OED study noted the high correlation between good supervision of the gender components and their satisfactory achievement. Good supervision

Box 2.3: Missed opportunities during supervision and ICR preparation in the Mexico Manpower Training Project (Ln. 2876)

The project aimed to retrain unemployed women as well as men. During implementation, an evaluation showed that women who had received training were less likely than men to find a job quickly or to receive a salary higher than in previous jobs. The 1994 project completion report noted these findings, stating that they would be addressed in the follow-up project, but did not include them in the "lessons learned" section. But the objectives of the follow-on Labor Market and Productivity Enhancement Project (Ln. 3542, approved 1993) paid special attention to women. While the staff appraisal report did not include any government assurances that gender issues would be given priority, it did promise other actions. The report:

- stated that women would benefit from the improvements to be introduced in the training programs and the reduction of labor market barriers that were keeping women from enjoying the full benefits of training;
- specified that studies would be conducted on the differential results of training for men and women, although these had been identified during the implementation of the first project;
- stated that an implementation plan would be drawn up for gender-related activities; and
- gave detailed specifications for collecting data and improving labor statistics but did not include any government assurances that gender issues would be given priority.

The Operations Evaluation Department mission that audited the first project looked at progress in the follow-up project, which was already in its third year of implementation. The audit found that the training provided for women had changed little since the problem was identified. The differential effects of the training program on women continued, and prospective employers often favored men in allocating scholarships. While data collected was gender-disaggregated, there was no evidence of any efforts to understand and counter the differential benefits for women and men reported in the project evaluation. At OED's suggestion, the regional office and borrower have agreed that someone with gender expertise should join the next supervision mission.

of the gender component, in turn, was also found to be related to the integration of gender goals with the main objectives of the project and to the inclusion of a social scientist or someone with gender expertise in the project team. For the 47 completed projects for which sufficient information is available, 9 benefited from good attention to gender issues during supervision, and 7 of these fully achieved their gender objectives. But only 9 of the 24 projects with no evidence of attention to gender during supervision achieved their gender objectives. The remaining 14 projects paid only superficial attention to gender.

Even projects with a clearly defined gender component may receive no (or only limited) attention during supervision and/or completion missions, however. Box 2.3 discusses a retraining program for displaced and unemployed workers in Mexico, using evidence from an OED audit mission conducted in April 1996.

Box 2.4: Missed opportunities in a recent implementation completion report

The documentation for the Uganda Program for Alleviation of Poverty and Social Costs of Adjustment (Cr. 2088) illustrates how old habits can be difficult to change. The 1996 implementation completion report (ICR) gives very little attention to gender issues in most of the program's components, although it does rate the single component that targeted women. This initiative—designed to provide war widows with improved access to health services and income-generating opportunities—was rated as unsatisfactory because it reached only 12 percent of the target group. The project staff appraisal report had identified the serious difficulties Ugandan women encountered in trying to obtain health and other services. The ICR discussion of gender in other components is limited to noting that some of the people receiving training were women and that health services were focusing more directly on maternal health.

Yet useful data on the impact of the program on men and on women were readily available, as a local firm had conducted a participatory evaluation of the program at project completion, at the Bank's request. In line with its terms of reference, the evaluation had looked at the impact of all program components on women and men. It concluded that program implementation would have been more effective if the population, including women, had been given a chance to influence some of the early decisions such as locations, types of equipment, and repayment rates. The evaluation makes a good case for integrating the views of both men and women in the design and process of this type of project. But the ICR made little use of the evidence, even though it refers to the evaluation. An Operations Evaluation Department audit confirmed the value of the participatory evaluation.

This weakness in the ICR is particularly noteworthy because it occurred for a country in which gender is generally well integrated in economic and sector work, most notably in the poverty assessment, the forthcoming case study of legal constraints to women's economic empowerment, and the preparatory work for the next country assistance strategy.

Coverage of gender issues in ICRs was uneven

Among the 58 completion documents available for review, implementation completion reports were more likely to mention gender in their review of implementation experience than earlier PCRs, but not systematically.[5] Although the standard format for Table 1 of the ICR annex includes a line for gender, almost half of the 36 ICRs that included the table stated that gender was "not applicable." This statement is understandable when the proposed gender-related action was very limited and could be discounted, yet the "not applicable" rating was also given for six projects in which one or more component specifically targeted women or for which gender aspects were highly relevant during implementation (whether identified in the SAR or not). Box 2.4 gives an example of such discrepancies.

This update shows, for the first time, that the outcome ratings for projects with gender-related action approved in FY87 and later compare favorably with the outcome for similar projects without gender actions: 74 percent of 54 projects with gender-related action in the agriculture and human resources sectors were rated satisfactory, against 65 percent for the 81 projects with similar sectoral distribution that did not include a gender-related action. The update also shows that the integration of gender objectives into project objectives is the most significant positive correlate with satisfactory gender outcomes. But the results of Bank projects related to gender issues remain difficult to evaluate, since project documents and files, including the supervision reports and ICRs, give only superficial attention to gender objectives and achievements.

Notes

1. This includes 24 projects for which the implementation completion reports or project completion reports (PCRs) had been reviewed and rated by the Operations Evaluation Department. For the remaining 34 projects, this chapter uses the self-evaluation ratings provided by the regional offices. These completed projects represent 84 percent of projects with gender-related action approved in FY87, with the proportion decreasing for more recent projects: 39 percent for projects approved in FY88, 28 percent for FY89, 19 percent for FY90, 9 percent for FY91, and 4 percent for FY92. None of the projects with gender-related action approved in or since FY93 had yet a PCR available even in draft. The total number of projects (58) is too small to yield results of high statistical significance for some variables. For example, only a few of the 58 projects included a good quality gender analysis, which makes it impossible to test the sample for association between good quality gender analysis and satisfactory achievement of gender objectives. Also, the relationship between total project outcome and achievement of the gender objective could not be assessed because all projects where gender objectives were achieved were also rated satisfactory.
2. This evolution is due in part to the change in the sectoral concentration of projects with gender-related action. The 1994 study had noted the heavy concentration of these projects in the agriculture sector, and especially in the area development subsector, where outcome ratings were lower than in other sectors and subsectors. The subsectoral categories of the management information system (MIS) have been changed since the 1994 OED study. The area development subsector was eliminated and the MIS database was retrofitted, with the old area development projects reassigned to various other subsectors. A comparison with the data in the 1994 gender study could not be made.
3. The implementation of seven of these projects was disrupted by civil war or other factors exogenous to the project.
4. A rating was assigned by OED to each project, from "0" (no attempt to identify gender roles) to "3" (a full gender analysis used to define objectives or strategies). There are too few cases for a meaningful discussion of the effects of gender analysis on this cluster. Good gender analysis was much more frequent in projects approved in FY94–95 (Chapter 3).
5. Since all these projects included gender-related actions, all completion documents should discuss them. Three of the 58 reports were drafts that task managers shared with OED before final review and printing, so the percentages given in this section are indicative only.

3. Gender in the investment portfolio

This chapter analyzes the features of projects with gender-related action approved in FY94, FY95, and FY96, for three purposes. The chapter seeks first to find out if the factors found to be associated with successful achievement of gender objectives are now more systematically present in the design of recently approved projects, and second, to further explore the possible link, noted in the 1994 study, between gender concerns and participatory approaches. The chapter then combines this new evidence with the data compiled for the 1994 study, to show how the prevalence and distribution of projects with gender-related action have evolved since FY87 across sectors and regions.

Features associated with the achievement of gender goals have become much more frequent in recent projects

Design quality in projects approved in FY94 and FY95

Features associated with successful achievement of the gender objectives (Chapter 2) have become significantly more frequent in projects approved in FY94 and FY95, and project design is generally of better quality than for projects approved in the late 1980s.

Gender analysis

Among the 120 projects with gender-related action approved in FY94 and FY95, only 14 (12 percent) showed no evidence of efforts to identify gender roles. This is a great improvement over the completed projects reviewed in Chapter 2, 67 percent of which included no gender analysis. Thirty-three of the recent projects included high-quality gender analysis that documented the productive, reproductive, and community roles of women and men in the project area and used this evidence to identify needs and appropriate strategies. Another 47 included substantial (though not thorough) gender analysis.[1] In the remaining 26 projects the gender analysis was superficial. Figures 3.1 and 3.2 show the increased prevalence and quality of gender analysis in recent projects compared with completed projects.

The incidence of projects with high- or substantial-quality gender analysis is greatest by far in the human resources sector and in the Africa (AFR) and the South Asia (SAS) regional offices. Figure 3.3 shows the breakdown of such projects across regions for the agriculture and human resources sectors.

When gender analysis was included, the findings were most often used to identify appropriate actions for strengthening women's productive roles (79 projects), community roles (51 projects), and reproductive roles (42 projects), with some projects focusing on more than one role. In all sectors, gender analysis was used most frequently to identify appropriate productive activities.

Box 3.1: The 1994 findings on gender prevalence, sectoral and regional distribution

The 1994 Operations Evaluation Department study showed a sharp increase in the prevalence of projects with gender-related actions started in FY87, which peaked in FY91. Projects with gender-related action were found mostly in the agriculture and the human resources sectors, and they increased most rapidly in the Africa region.

The argument used most frequently (in 72 out of 120 projects) to justify gender-related activities was equity—that is, ensuring that women as well as men benefited from project activities. Poverty arguments were used in 53 projects and welfare arguments in 40, but economic efficiency was explicitly used in only 30 cases. Some projects addressed more than one rationale. These findings contrast with the 58 completed projects reviewed in the previous chapter, which used only two arguments to justify gender objectives: productive efficiency and improving the welfare of women. The Bank's 1994 internal policy paper based its arguments for strengthening the role of WID on economic efficiency and equity. The fact that task managers are now more likely to use an equity argument to justify including some gender-related action in their projects is thus in line with Bank policy. This development parallels changes in other development agencies and the Development Assistance Committee (DAC) of the Organization for Economic Cooperation and Development (OECD) (see Chapter 5).

Gender objectives and their integration into project objectives

OED's 1994 study noted that gender objectives were becoming better integrated into project objectives. This trend is confirmed in the FY94–95 projects, as 85 of the 120 projects showed such integration. This evolution is significant, given that projects are more likely to meet their gender objectives when these objectives are well articulated and integrated into project objectives (Chapter 2).

All 33 of the FY94–95 projects with high-quality gender analysis integrated their gender objectives into their overall project objectives. Only 4 of the 14 projects with no gender analysis can make this claim. For example, the Guinea Equity and School Improvement Project (Cr. 2719) had as one of its goals increasing girls' enrollment in primary schools. During project preparation, gender analysis showed that parents gave much weight to proximity to home, safety, and adequate sanitation facilities when deciding whether to send their girls to school. The project components were designed to respond to these findings: smaller, multigrade classrooms would be built close to individual communities, adequate sanitary facilities would be included in all schools, and parents would be involved in the upkeep and maintenance of the schools. By integrating the special needs of girls in project design, the schools have adapted to parents' concerns and so are likely to serve the community better.

The strategy used most frequently (in 102 projects) to reach gender objectives involved targeting services to women users or clients. Targets ranged from all women farmers in a project area to more restricted categories of clients. Quantified goals were rarely specified. Thirty-five projects also planned to hire women to provide services tailored to women and girls. But quotas specifying the percentage of clients who must be women were used infre-

FIGURE 3.1: GENDER ANALYSIS IN 58 COMPLETED PROJECTS APPROVED FY87–91

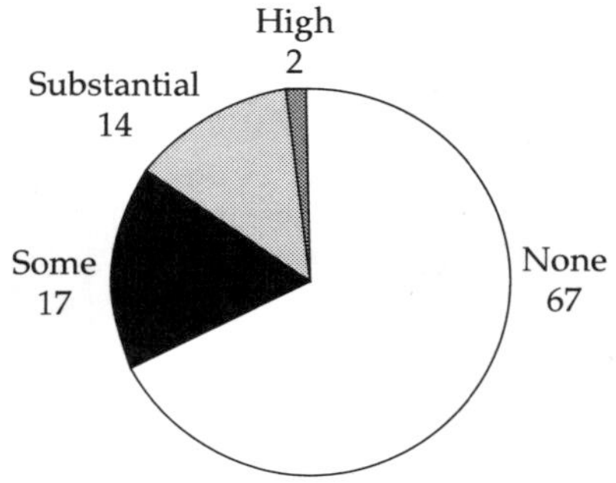

Source: OED.

FIGURE 3.2: GENDER ANALYSIS IN 120 PROJECTS APPROVED FY94–95

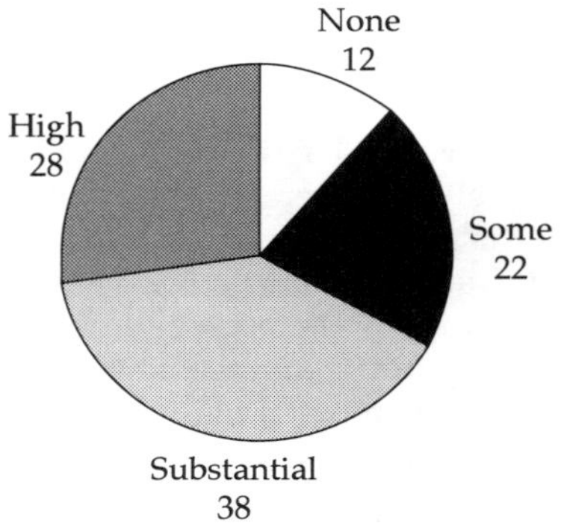

Source: OED.

FIGURE 3.3: PERCENTAGES OF HIGH- OR SUBSTANTIAL-QUALITY GENDER ANALYSIS IN PROJECTS WITH GENDER-RELATED ACTION APPROVED IN FY94 AND FY95, BY REGIONAL OFFICE

(agricultural and human resources sectors)[a]

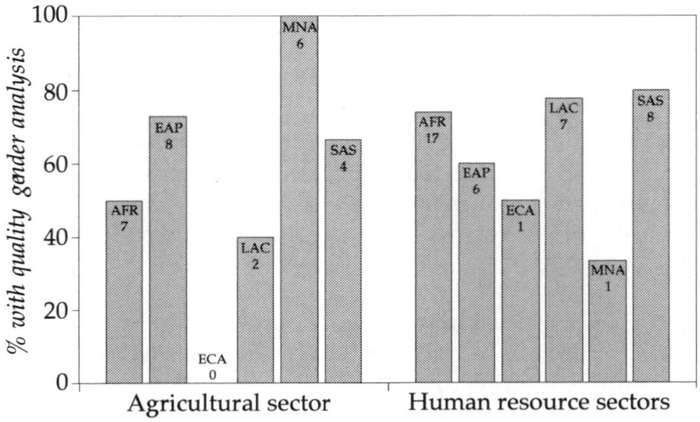

a. Numbers for other sectors are too small to permit meaningful regional percentages.
Source: OED.

Box 3.2: Promising practices: the integration of gender into project supervision and monitoring and evaluation

The *Sri Lanka Poverty Alleviation Project* (Cr. 2231, approved in FY91) seeks to increase income-generating opportunities among the poor and to improve the nutritional status of children under three and of pregnant and lactating mothers. The midterm supervision report tracks levels of women's participation in credit and microenterprise activities, nutrition interventions and community works, and activities related to the mobilization of the poor. Although hampered by the lack of projectwide gender-disaggregated data, the review team was able to identify desirable changes in strategy, demonstrating its commitment to gender concerns in the project.

quently (seven cases). Such narrow targeting requires more detailed knowledge of the characteristics, needs, and preferences of potential users. Experience may show that narrow targeting is more likely when a high-quality gender analysis has been done.

Projects approved in FY94–95 have a higher quality gender analysis and are more likely to integrate gender into overall project goals

Implementation

Overall, the projects approved in FY94–95 have a higher quality of gender analysis and are more likely to integrate gender objectives into overall project objectives than the projects approved in earlier years. Since these factors have been linked to successful implementation in completed projects, this evolution is encouraging. By themselves, however, gender analysis and gender-related objectives do not guarantee that implementation and outcomes will be successful or even that gender will receive enough attention during implementation, supervision, and evaluation. Box 3.2 describes a promising use of supervision findings.

Links between gender issues and other Bank concerns

In recent years, the Bank has promoted the use of participatory approaches at all phases of the project cycle and in ESW.[2] The 120 projects with gender-related action approved in FY94 and FY95 were rated for the level of participation during design or the level planned for implementation, using the typology now favored throughout the Bank of no participation, information, consultation, and collaboration with stakeholders. Only 4 of the 120 projects did not mention promoting participation at any level, but 37 planned to seek full collaboration with some key stakeholders and combined a participatory approach with gender-related action. Of course, no conclusion on causality can be drawn from this data, but any link between gender and participatory approaches provides the Bank and borrowers with opportunities for mutually reinforcing efforts in these two areas of concern. (See Box 3.3 for some examples of projects with participatory design and gender-related objectives.)

The 37 projects seeking collaboration were found mostly in AFR (which has a larger number of projects overall) and the Latin America and the Caribbean regional office (LAC) (Figure 3.4). The agriculture sector had 21 such projects, followed by 10 in human resources (Figure 3.5).

Thirteen of the 120 projects combine a high level of gender analysis with a collaborative approach to participation that truly gives beneficiaries a voice

Box 3.3: Promising practices: participatory design for gender objectives

The *Pakistan Social Action Program (Cr. 2593)* involves parents in its efforts to increase the enrollment of girls in primary and secondary schools. Parents have been participating in school and rural water supply programs, and parents' committees now oversee government schools in Balochistan. Many communities without schools have been encouraged to build their own schools and to hire female teachers, who will be paid by the government.

A subproject component in the *Ecuador Third Social Development Project: Social Investment Fund (Ln. 3707)* finances actions in primary health and education, basic infrastructure, and small-scale productive community investments under an emergency social investment fund. Because women and households headed by women will be the primary beneficiaries, they are actively involved in the design, implementation, and maintenance of these activities.

in decisions affecting their lives. Eight of these projects are in the human resources sector; one is a social investment fund project listed in the social sector, and the remaining four are in the agriculture sector. The diversity of projects in this innovative category is striking: they include health projects in Croatia (Ln. 3843), Peru (Ln. 3701), and Panama (Ln. 3841); population and human resources in Comoros (Cr. 2553); general education in Mauritania (Cr. 2706); irrigation in Morocco (Ln. 3688); food security in Benin (Cr. 2601); micro- and small-enterprise training in Kenya (Cr. 2596); forest management and conservation in Lao (Cr. 2586); a social investment fund in Ecuador (Ln. 3707); a social recovery project in Zambia (Cr. 2755); a poverty reduction project in China (Southwest, Cr. 2744); and an equity and school improvement project in Guinea (Cr. 2719).

Regional offices recently chose 19 of their "flagship" participatory ESW reports or projects for periodic reporting to the President. Many of these projects are just being prepared (one was approved in FY93), so they are not part of the 120 new projects reviewed in this chapter. Given the possible link between attention to gender issues and participatory approaches, OED reviewed the files of the 19 flagship projects. Several give clear evidence of excellent integration of gender issues, for example, the Armenia Social Investment Fund (Cr. 2784) and the Balochistan Primary Education Project in Pakistan (Cr. 2482). But others show no evidence of attention to gender, even though gender issues are relevant to the project objectives.

The human resources and agricultural sectors account for 79 percent of all investment projects with gender-related action approved between FY94 and FY96

Evolution of the portfolio with gender-related action, FY87–96

The previous two sections compared the design features of projects recently approved with those approved from FY87–93. A significant improvement in quality and an increasing link between gender concerns and participatory approaches has been established. This success can now be assessed against the first three principles of the Bank's 1994 strategy, that is, focus on education, health, labor, agriculture, and financial services; concentration in countries where the need is greatest; and more general mainstreaming of gender into Bank work (described in Box 1.1). This section first compares the sectoral and regional distributions of projects with gender-related action with those of the total investment portfolio approved from FY87–96, and then combines all portfolio data to show how the prevalence of projects with gender-related action has evolved.

FIGURE 3.4: LEVEL OF PARTICIPATION IN PROJECTS WITH GENDER-RELATED ACTION, BY REGIONAL OFFICE

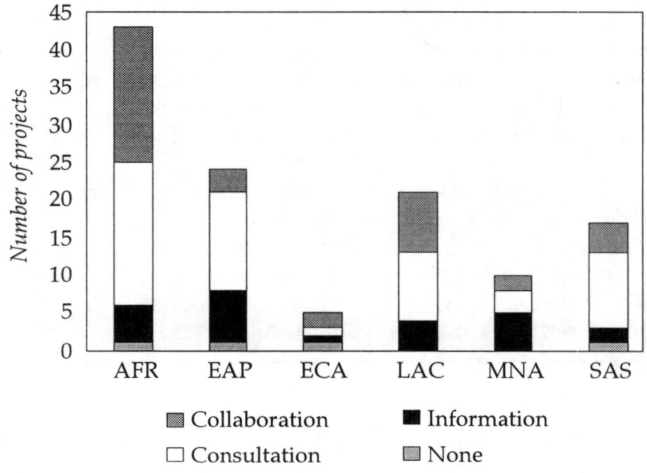

Source: OED.

FIGURE 3.5: DISTRIBUTION OF PARTICIPATORY EFFORTS IN PROJECTS WITH GENDER-RELATED ACTION, BY SECTOR

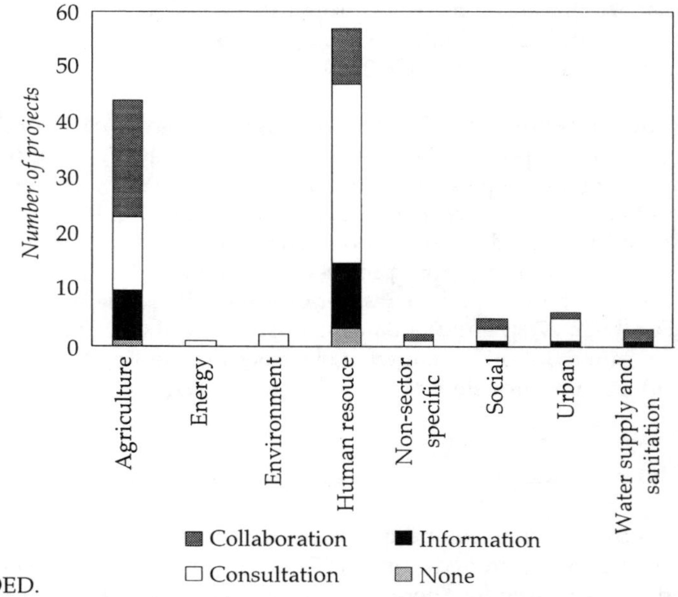

Source: OED.

Sectoral distribution

The 1994 gender policy, like the WID work program of the previous six years, calls for concentrating the Bank's efforts on girls' education, women's health, agriculture, labor markets, and financial services. Figure 3.6 shows that, in line with Bank priorities, the human resources[3] and agriculture[4] sectors together account for 79 percent of all investment projects that include

FIGURE 3.6: DISTRIBUTION OF PROJECTS WITH GENDER-RELATED ACTIONS ACROSS SECTORS, FY94, FY95, AND FY96
(percent)

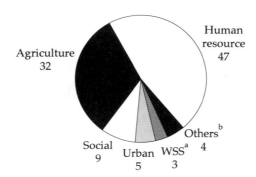

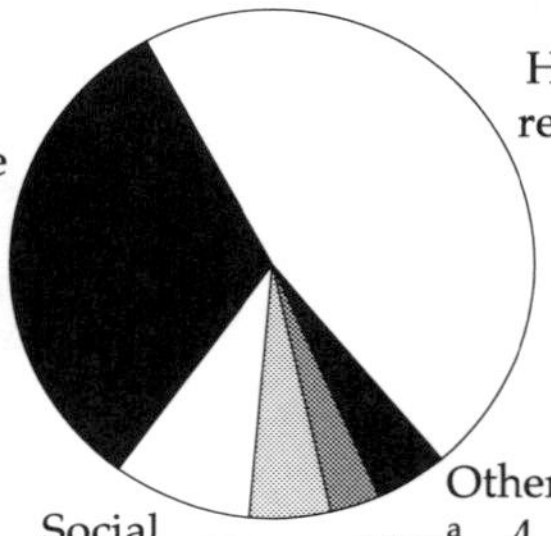

Note: The Bank management information system created a new category of "social sector" projects in FY94. Most projects in this category would have been classified as human resources under the previous system. None of the projects formally classified in the financial sector included gender-related actions.
a. WSS = Water supply and sanitation.
b. "Others" includes transportation, energy, industry, environment, and nonspecific sectors.
Sources: World Bank management information system; OED.

gender-related action approved between FY94 and FY96. But actions that promote integration of gender issues in relation with labor markets and financial services were often found in projects classified in the MIS as human resources or agriculture sectors, so there is more diversity across all of the 1994 policy priorities than shown in this data. Nevertheless, the draft regional action plans, while emphasizing the five areas cited in the gender policy, also identify the need for gender-related actions in areas such as transport (Africa), social security and services (Europe and Central Asia regional office, or ECA), and public sector modernization (LAC). Recent Bank studies, such as a case study on the role of women (Malmberg-Calvo 1994), *Confronting Crisis* (Moser 1996), and a tool kit on women and water and sanitation projects (Fong, Wakeman, and Bhushan 1996), show how gender concerns are increasingly found in a diversity of sectors.

Distribution across countries

As noted in the 1994 study, the investment portfolios for low-income countries[5] continue to include a greater proportion of projects with gender-related action than the portfolios for low-, middle-, and high-income countries. From FY94–96, about 40 percent of projects approved in low-income countries included some gender-related action. In low- to middle-income countries, however, only 13 percent of projects in FY94 and 23 percent of projects in FY95 and FY96 incorporated such actions. Overall, about two-thirds of all projects with gender-related action approved each year (501 out of the 802 approved between FY67 and FY96) are in low-income countries.

About two-thirds of all projects with gender-related action approved each year are in low-income countries

The relative proportion of projects with gender-related action in each region's portfolio is therefore influenced in part by the number of low-income countries in the area. A significant jump (more than double) in the number of projects with gender-related action occurs after FY88 for AFR and

The number of projects with gender-related actions more than doubled for most regions in FY88–89

the East Asia and Pacific regional office (EAP) and after FY89 for LAC and SAS (Figure 3.7). Despite some yearly variations, the levels of the late 1980s are being maintained, but they are not rising.

The 1994 internal policy paper mandates that Bank lending for gender-related activities be focused on countries and areas where underinvestment in women has been acute. For this update, OED identified countries where the

FIGURE 3.7: INVESTMENT PROJECTS WITH GENDER-RELATED ACTION AS A PERCENTAGE OF THE INVESTMENT PORTFOLIO ACROSS REGIONS, APPROVED FY83–96

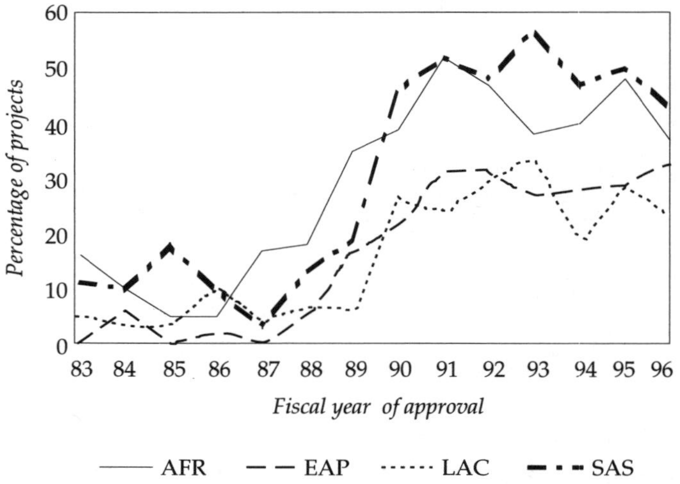

Note: The Middle East and North Africa and Europe and Central Asia regional offices have not been considered because of the relatively small number of projects involved.
Sources: World Bank management information system; OED.

FIGURE 3.8: PROJECTS WITH GENDER-RELATED ACTION, TOTAL INVESTMENT PORTFOLIO APPROVED IN FY87–96[a]

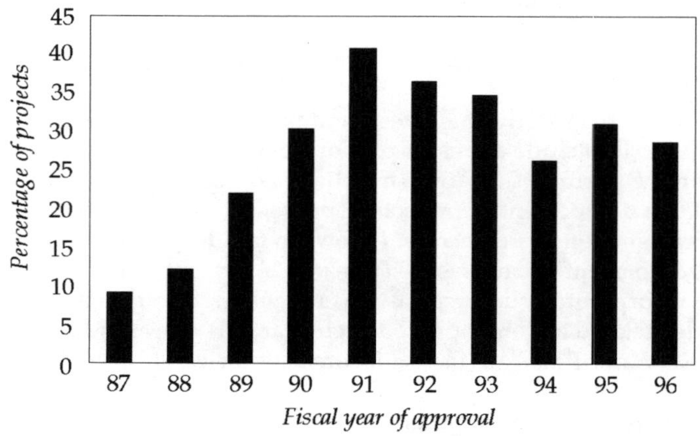

a. Excluding loans for structural adjustment, sectoral adjustment, and debt reduction.
Sources: World Bank gender analysis and poverty team; OED.

gender gap is greatest, as measured by four health and education indicators: life expectancy, maternal mortality, literacy, and access to education.[6] The 12 countries that rank lowest on at least three of these four indicators are, by Bank regional office: Comoros, Guinea, Malawi, Senegal, Sudan, and Uganda (AFR); Bangladesh, Bhutan, India, and Pakistan (SAS); Yemen (Middle East and North Africa Regional Office [MNA]); and Papua New Guinea (EAP).

For all 12 countries, 85 of the 1,124 investment projects (8 percent) approved between FY67 and FY86 included some gender-related actions, a proportion similar to that found for the investment portfolio worldwide. For projects approved between FY87 and FY93, the proportion jumped to 32 percent (129 projects with gender-related action out of 409 investment projects), slightly above the overall portfolio. Between FY94 and FY96, the proportion increased again to 41 percent (58 projects out of 141 approved), well above the 26–31 percent range for the entire portfolio. These 12 countries show a higher level of attention to gender issues than the entire investment portfolio, an indication that the mandate to concentrate on countries with the greatest gender gap is being implemented.

Distribution by approval year

The annual proportion of projects with gender-related action among investment projects varied around 30 percent in the past three years (Figure 3.8). This is below the peak years of FY91–93, but well above the 10 to 20 percent of the late 1980s. The higher design quality of gender actions in recent projects means that overall, the gender quality of the portfolio has improved, and gender is addressed through projects with broader objectives rather than through WID-only projects,[7] in line with Bank policy. But can gender be considered mainstreamed in the investment portfolio?[8] This is a difficult question to answer, since gender concerns are not present equally across sectors and countries, and since the Bank has set no quantitative targets.

The great variation found across sectors (see section on sectoral distribution) can help establish some rough estimates of realistic goals for mainstreaming. Gender concerns are pervasive in health, population, and nutrition and social sectors, and they are likely to be relevant in most educational and many agricultural projects. Recent Bank work has also recognized the importance of gender in such areas as labor regulations, pensions, and other social policy issues (especially in Eastern Europe), and transport. Hypothetical targets of 80–90 percent in the health, population, and nutrition and social sectors, 70–80 percent in education, 60–70 percent in agriculture, and 20–30 percent in finances, urban, and water would result in an overall ceiling of 40–45 percent if the sectoral composition of the portfolio was as found in FY96. The composition of the portfolio may change in ways that would raise that ceiling. First, those sectors where gender is most relevant, such as human resources and agriculture, are expected to increase their share of the portfolio in the next few years. Second, as some of the high- to middle-income countries "graduate," the Bank will be able to concentrate on poorer countries and those with the greatest gender gaps.

Although design quality of gender-related actions has improved, the proportion of projects with such actions remains low

Although design quality of gender-related actions has improved in recent years, the proportion of projects with such actions and effective gender analysis remains low. Even in the human resources sector, the 24 projects with high-quality gender analysis represent only 28 percent of the 86 projects approved in FY95 and FY96. No single reason explains the scattered incidence of good design—the best cases are spread over all regions and many sectors. But high-quality gender analysis is clearly associated with the use of participatory approaches during project preparation.

Notes

1. The rating used for completed projects was also applied to the new projects to determine the presence and level of gender analysis in project staff appraisal reports, from "0" (no attempt to understand gender roles) to "3" (full gender analysis leading to definition of objectives or strategy).
2. Events that could have influenced task managers during the review period included workshops on participation in February 1992 and May 1994, a Board presentation of a report on the World Bank and participation in September 1994, followed by implementation of participation action plans in each region and central vice presidency, meetings with the Interagency Group on Participation in September 1995 and March 1996, and the involvement of many task managers in the preparation of the *World Bank Participation Sourcebook* (World Bank 1995g).
3. Projects in the population, health, and nutrition sector and, to a lesser degree, education projects are by their nature likely to include some activities directly targeted at women or girls. The importance of girls' education is mentioned and leads to specific action in over half (53 percent) of education projects. Among subsectors, population and nutrition are the only ones in which all projects approved in the past five years have included some gender-related actions.
4. The high concentration of projects with gender-related actions in the agriculture and rural development sector is due in part to the weight of the Africa regional office (AFR), which accounts for 69 percent of all such projects. Women are very much involved in agricultural work throughout most of the countries in AFR and are therefore difficult to ignore. Nevertheless, even in AFR, only 66 percent of agricultural projects approved in FY94 and FY95 included some gender-related action, usually in the form of measures to ensure access to information and services.
5. Countries with per capita incomes of $695 or less (World Bank 1995f).
6. Based on United Nations 1995. The four indicators (1990–95) used as evidence of the gap between men and women are: an advantage for women in life expectancy of only two years or less, a female mortality ratio of more than 300 per 100,00 live births, a difference in male and female illiteracy rates for those age 15–24 of more than 16 percent, and a secondary school enrollment ratio for women of 60 per 100 men or below.
7. The Gambia Women in Development (WID) Project (Cr. 2141) is still under implementation. The Côte d'Ivoire WID Pilot Project (Ln. 3251) was recently completed. There were no other WID-only projects during the period under review. (A WID project in Mexico was canceled.)
8. Chapter 4 discusses the mainstreaming of gender in economic and sector work and country assistance strategies.

4. Gender in nonlending services

The 1994 internal gender policy mandates that gender be integrated into economic and sector work and country assistance strategies whenever appropriate. But reports prepared by Bank management in response to the OED ledger of recommendations, and more recently to brief CODE, recognize that while many country assistance strategies identify some gender issues, most do not discuss possible strategies. This chapter assesses recent evidence that the earlier WID assessments contributed to subsequent lending and nonlending work, and that gender is becoming more systematically integrated in ESW and CASs, at least in the 12 countries where the need is greatest.

The legacy of WID assessments in the late 1980s

Some WID assessments were superficial and did not influence subsequent work. Others (for example, India, Pakistan, and Turkey) played a key role in promoting active, ongoing dialogues with the borrowers. Good sector work provides a solid basis for project design and helps clarify with borrowers the issues that can best be addressed with Bank assistance. For example, a 1989 WID assessment for the Philippines noted the country's relatively high fertility and mortality rates and brought women's health issues to the attention of Bank staff. A sector report was prepared to assess the country's population program. This report was instrumental in the government's decision to adopt a health rationale for family planning and to give priority to a women's health and safe motherhood project. Similarly, the origins of the China Southwest Poverty Reduction Project (Cr. 2744), which contains extensive measures to increase women's labor mobility, can be traced to the preparation and public release of a 1992 Bank study that made poverty reduction a more explicit focus of Bank lending in China.

Good ESW provides a solid basis for project design and helps clarify with borrowers issues that can best be addressed with Bank assistance

Early economic and sector work, especially the WID assessments, often identified bottlenecks in legal and regulatory frameworks and policies that hampered women's access to resources and services. As a result, several projects approved in FY94–95 attempted policy, administrative, or legal reforms that would affect women. For example, the Pakistan Social Action Program Project (Cr. 2593) proposes policy reforms to address systemic problems in primary education, including allowing girls to attend boys' schools and vice versa; relaxing age and qualification requirements to increase the number of female teachers in rural areas; in Balochistan, amending rules so that both men and women can apply for positions previously restricted to men and retired teachers; and in the Northwest Frontier Province, revising service rules to allow the hiring of local girls to be trained as teachers by mobile units. In the Mauritania General Education Project (Cr. 2706), policy and administrative measures are planned to promote female education. These measures would include allowing communities and schools greater authority to set the

Box 4.1: The 1994 findings on women in development (WID) assessments

The Operations Evaluation Department study showed that the systematic preparation of country-level WID assessments, which were required from all regional offices in the late 1980s, strengthened gender work in several ways. At the country level it helped the Bank identify relevant issues, and incorporate them into the dialogue between the Bank and borrowers. The process also highlighted generic issues found in many countries, such as the importance of legal and regulatory factors in determining women's access to services and labor opportunities.

Box 4.2: Promising practices: gender issues in sector work

Common issues across countries. "Rural Women in the Sahel and their Access to Agricultural Extension" (World Bank 1995c) documents women's pivotal role in the economy of rural areas with high levels of poverty and fragile agroclimatic environments. It discusses how extension services can better meet women's needs, and some of the measures it proposes are already being implemented. In the same vein, *Girls and Schools in Sub-Saharan Africa: From Analysis to Action* (Odaga and Heneveld 1995) documents the issues and possible actions in a priority topic.

Women's situation in one country. A recent survey in Indonesia showed that labor regulations are not all fully applied to women workers in the manufacturing sector and that women were not all aware of their rights. With Bank support, a local nongovernmental organization (NGO) is now informing women of these regulations. A broader review of the legal framework and the constraints that women may encounter has also been conducted.

Women in one sector in one country. "Financial Services for the Rural Poor and Women in India: Access and Sustainability" (Mahajan and Ramola 1996) analyzes how well financial institutions reach the rural poor, especially women. Based on this and a review of experience in other countries (Bennett and Goldberg 1996), a survey of six hundred households below the poverty line was conducted to map the demand for and supply of financial services among poor men and women in two districts in North India. The study identified a hierarchy of constraints and developed a package of reforms for the rural financial sector.

Country strategy. An internal study highlights the contribution women make to Moroccan society and identifies the constraints that limit their productivity, income, and social welfare. The study proposes a program to address poverty and gender concerns at the country level.

Gender issues across sectors. "El Salvador—Moving to a Gender Approach: Issues and Recommendations" (World Bank 1995b) identifies gender issues in health, education, labor, land tenure, credit, rural water, and energy. This report documents differences in the roles of men and women and examines gender differentials in access to resources and services. It distinguishes behavioral differences—such as tastes and preferences—from inequities caused by gender discrimination. The report proposes goals, sets out an action program, and identifies local NGOs qualified to help implement the plan.

school calendar to accommodate children's work requirements; increasing to 50 percent the share of female secondary scholarship recipients; and increasing the number of women in management positions in the Ministry of Education. In the Uganda Institutional Capacity Building Project (Cr. 2736), laws relating to domestic relations are being amended under the Law Reform Exercise. These laws affect the rights of women, their position within society, and their ability to engage independently in commercial and economic activity.

Gender in recent economic and sector work

In 1994, OED recommended various steps to better integrate gender into country and sector work as well as the portfolio, such as bringing in gender expertise during ESW and formally including gender in discussions with the borrowers. In recent years, a diversity of ways to incorporate gender issues in sector work has emerged, mostly through a systematic documentation and analysis of women's roles and potentials (Box 4.2).

The 1994 study also recommended that proposals seeking to increase attention to gender be considered for financing through FIAHS, a matching grant fund established in 1994 to improve the quality of Bank operations in areas that have yet to be mainstreamed into the Bank's operational work. During FY95, a $2 million replenishment supported several initiatives related to gender issues (Box 4.3). Many of these activities served to provide a more thorough and location-specific understanding of how gender issues relate to development choices.

Gender in country assistance strategies

Progress in integrating gender aspects in CASs has been slow

The 1994 OED study recommended that country departments determine what steps, if any, are needed to ensure that the required CAS statement on gender reflects a good understanding of the situation and contributes to the policy discussion with member countries. Management agreed to do so. Management reports that 52 of the 100 assistance strategies prepared during FY94 and FY95 specifically discussed gender issues, with the CASs for India, Indonesia, Madagascar, Malawi, Panama, and Zambia given as good examples. A review of these strategy papers and the evidence from the 12 countries with the greatest gender gap (identified in the section on distribution across countries) shows that progress in integrating gender aspects in CAS work (throughout the CAS preparation as well as in the document itself) has been slow.

Country assistance strategies have been issued since 1993 for all 12 countries with the greatest gap except Sudan, and poverty assessments have been completed for 9 of them. The CASs were reviewed to identify relevant gender issues, discussions of priorities and possible strategies, breakdowns of key indicators for men and women, and utilization of gender findings from the poverty assessment (if available). The section also draws from the proposed action plans that the regions are finalizing.[1]

The 1994 OED study identified Bangladesh, India, and Pakistan as countries that had high-quality WID assessments and had made good progress in integrating gender in their lending portfolio. These three countries were also the first to have local staff at the Bank mission assigned to work specifically on gender issues, and in each case, staff with strong personal commitment and field experience have been involved in sector and lending work since the

Box 4.3: Examples of Fund for Innovative Approaches in Human and Social Development (FIAHS) funding for innovative work on gender issues

Studies for economic and sector work. One of the five studies carried out as part of the sector report on improving education in Pakistan analyzes the possible influence of community participation on girls' education. The study used the fund to cover the collection of data, both qualitative and quantitative, that would identify whether and how community participation made a difference in the schools.

Fieldwork during project preparation. In Pakistan, FIAHS funds were used in the Balochistan Primary Education Project and sector work. Together with matched supervision funds from the project and the education sector work budget, they supported social assessment to improve understanding of community organization and capacity building in Balochistan. The study, which will influence Bank strategy in Pakistan, helped strengthen local evaluative capacity. FIAHS funds will be used for the forthcoming midterm review.

Poverty monitoring. FIAHS funds supported a participatory workshop on poverty monitoring and analysis held in South Africa. Participants were from nongovernmental organizations, government departments, universities, businesses, and labor. The workshop clearly brought out that women—in the words of one participant—work in the "survival sector." The workshop also stressed the importance of building a partnership among organizations and poor people to work on policy and program design, implementation, and monitoring.

early 1990s. This update confirms that gender issues are addressed effectively in each country, although with differing emphases.

The 1996 CASs for Bangladesh and Pakistan stand out for their thorough attention to gender in all variables, including their utilization of findings from the poverty assessments. The two countries are already implementing projects with innovative strategies for reaching girls and women, and especially for ensuring that parents keep their girls as well as their boys in school. The pattern established in earlier years is being sustained, and a review of the country general files confirms that, for Bangladesh, gender is well integrated into Bank work (Box 4.3).

The 1996 country assistance strategies for Bangladesh and Pakistan stand out for their thorough attention to gender

The 1994 study also noted the high-quality WID assessment prepared for India in 1991. The CAS currently under implementation refers to gender issues but does not discuss them in terms of priorities or strategies (it does provide gender-disaggregated data). However, quality work on gender issues was done in sector work and studies, especially for the health, education, and financial services sectors. The action plan for SAS reflects excellent ongoing gender work in the poverty assessment for India and in the preparation of a rural finance project (an innovative, free-standing project for rural women) and the next CAS.

The CASs for the other countries in the Asia regions with the greatest gender gap (Bhutan, Comoros, and Papua New Guinea) include only a limited treatment of gender.[2] The two CASs for Bhutan and Comoros (both issued in 1993, before the gender policy was issued) are included in a project memorandum to the president (MOP)—for the Third Forestry Development Project and a population and human resources project, respectively. The CASs refer to the needs of women but do not discuss strategies, even in the context of the project they are linked with. The CAS for Bhutan identifies the need to improve women's access to educational, health, and agricultural services, and the MOP states that the forestry project will enhance women's role in decisions involving environmental issues. The CAS for Comoros (prepared before a poverty assessment was completed) mentions the needs of girls and women in relation to education and health access but does not discuss priorities or gender strategies.

In MNA, the 1994 study noted that Yemen stood out for its strong discussion of WID issues in its latest country economic memorandum, which drew from a series of WID-action projects in education and agriculture and a WID strategy paper. The FY96 CAS clearly links gender concerns with the development priority areas of population, education, and maternal and child health, a link which was well documented in the poverty assessment. The need to involve women in other sectors, while not highlighted in the CAS, is integrated in subsequent lending (TAIZ Water Supply Pilot Project).

In Africa, Malawi, Uganda, Senegal, and Guinea all improved their handling of gender issues

In Africa, the four countries with low gender indicators have all improved their handling of gender issues since the 1994 study. Drawing from the poverty assessments, the country assistance strategies for Malawi (FY96) and Uganda (FY95) prioritize and effectively discuss gender issues. The CAS for Senegal (FY95) also identifies (but does not prioritize) gender issues. The Guinea CAS (FY94) is more superficial in its treatment of gender issues, perhaps because it is presented within a health and nutrition sector project (Box 4.4).

Box 4.4: Incorporating gender in country strategy: recent examples

Incorporating gender in the country dialogue. A review of the Bank's general files for Bangladesh in the year preceding publication of the country assistance strategy (CAS) showed that managers and staff at the resident mission and in Washington referred to gender aspects frequently and routinely in both formal exchanges with the borrower and informal exchanges between the mission and the headquarters.

Utilization of poverty assessment findings in the CAS. The task manager for the Uganda poverty assessment used participatory methods that allowed the poor, including children and women, to share their understanding of poverty and wealth. This early example of a participatory poverty assessment included a thorough discussion of differences in men's and women's access to goods and services and discussed the gender consequences of civil strife. The CAS (issued in May 1995) used these findings to identify gender issues and devise appropriate priorities and strategies. The CAS's gender focus contrasts with the limited attention given to gender in projects recently completed in Uganda (Chapter 3).

Sectoral bias. The Guinea country assistance strategy was written in conjunction with a health and nutrition sector project and limits its discussion of gender to girls' education. The CAS's paragraph on areas of special emphasis notes that women constitute a large majority of Guinea's rural labor force but are excluded from rights to property and credit. The CAS further notes that the long-term implications of their limited access to health care and education are enormous. But the CAS discusses general issues in employment, agriculture, land tenure, and legislation without mentioning gender concerns. Despite the superficial treatment of gender in the CAS, the current portfolio includes excellent plans to improve educational opportunities for girls.

The total package of gender efforts —in ESW, studies, the CAS, and project documents— is what truly reflects progress toward mainstreaming

The CASs for these 12 countries differ in their approach to gender issues. Generally, more recent strategies treat gender issues more thoroughly than earlier ones. But there is no clear pattern within individual countries to show the evolution from early economic and sector work to CASs and then to lending. In countries where the issues are particularly relevant, this diversity shows that attention to gender is not yet systematically integrated into the preparation of CASs. India's experience shows that CASs cannot be used in isolation to assess whether gender is mainstreamed in Bank work and in the dialogue with the borrower. Rather, it is the package of gender efforts in ESW, studies that focus specifically on gender, the CAS, and individual project documents that truly reflect progress toward mainstreaming.

These findings coincide with those presented to management by the Task Group on Social Development. Both sets of findings underscored the lack of attention to social factors in country and sector work. The task group has recommended that each region select two or three CASs and systematically integrate social concerns, including gender issues, into them. Current efforts toward participatory approaches to CAS preparation, project preparation, and project implementation should help identify and prioritize gender issues.

As a rule, the regional draft action plans advocate the systematic integration of gender issues into ESW and the CAS preparation, with country-level assessments of gender priorities a key objective. The action plans make a clear distinction between this desirable goal and a perfunctory statement on gender that is not based on a thorough assessment of needs.

Notes

1. Action plans for the East Asia and Pacific and South Asia regional offices were presented at a gender symposium, November 12–14, 1996. The action plans for the other regions were still in draft at the time of writing.
2. In Papua New Guinea, serious macroeconomic and structural problems have tended to dwarf other concerns. The East Asia and Pacific action plan now proposes a gender specialist who will work with Bank and borrower staff in Papua New Guinea.

5. Gender in a changing Bank

Beyond Beijing

Activities linked to the 1995 Beijing Conference on Women led governments, NGOs, and development agencies to take stock of their approach to gender issues (Chapter 1). This stocktaking comes at a time when women are finding common ground across cultures and economic status in spite of great differences in their relative positions and the tremendous disparity between well-off and poor women (Sivard 1995).

Four themes run through the experience of the Bank (as reviewed in chapters 2 to 4) and other development agencies: (1) gender issues are relevant to development for equity reasons; (2) good gender analysis is essential; (3) attention is shifting from projects to country programs; and (4) clear targets and specific action plans are needed. Following the lead established in Beijing, many agencies are now justifying attention to gender on grounds of equity—and in a few cases of empowerment—thus broadening the earlier, narrower focus on economic efficiency and poverty alleviation. For example, the gender action framework[1] of the Development Assistance Committee of the OECD countries clearly states that its goals are human rights and equity, not the integration of women into the development process. The DAC's strategic objective is gender equality in the context of sustainable, people-centered development. The report illustrates this point, noting that both men and women in equal partnership take the responsibility to define the development agenda, set the vision and goals, and develop strategies. The Canadian International Development Agency's (CIDA) 1995 policy on women in development and gender equity goes beyond its 1984 policy's emphasis on women as agents and beneficiaries of development to an emphasis on gender equity and women's empowerment. Similarly, the Bank's overarching focus on poverty reduction justifies attention to gender aspects on the basis of equity as well as economic efficiency.

The Bank's overarching focus on poverty reduction justifies attention to gender aspects on the basis of equity as well as economic efficiency

The 1994 OED study noted the Bank's role in developing the concept of gender analysis during the early 1980s. The importance of effective gender analysis during project design is now generally recognized, and many agencies have developed guidelines for their staff on scope and methodology. Generally, these guidelines share several points that are relevant to the Bank: the importance of looking at both men's and women's roles; the recognition that women do not form a homogeneous group within a given country or culture; the need to look beyond productive activities to family and community tasks; and the need to analyze intrahousehold decision processes.

In the early years of WID concerns, the focus was mostly on bringing women into development activities at the project level. In the Bank, the WID assessments begun in the late 1980s initiated the shift toward country-level analy-

Box 5.1: 1994 Operations Evaluation Department recommendations on institutional support: steady progress

The 1994 study recommended a more systematic involvement of staff with gender skills in economic and sector work and project work; stronger promotion and use of sex-disaggregated data; and financial support for innovative approaches under the Fund for Innovative Approaches in Human and Social Development (FIAHS), which had just been approved as the study was concluded. The strong increase in quality and frequency of sound gender analysis certainly indicates that staff or consultants with good gender skills (who need not be gender specialists) intervene more systematically in project preparation. Similarly, sex-disaggregated data were included more frequently, but not yet systematically, in country assistance strategies and project documents. OED impact evaluations also document gender impact more systematically. The FIAHS funds were used for activities that supported good gender integration in sector and project work, and several regions set up matching funds for gender work. Overall, progress is clear, but the focus groups with task managers show a strong demand for further training and technical support and for clearer recognition of their efforts.

ses of gender concerns that are now expected in all CASs. The DAC has also stated that the focus on WID must be broadened to include programs and country-level strategies. Many of the bilateral aid agencies and regional development banks have issued detailed gender action plans establishing gender priorities and targets, a step now almost completed in the Bank.

Institutional support for gender in the Bank

The 1994 OED study highlighted the strong increase in institutional support for mainstreaming gender after FY87—the proactive years—that has been demonstrated in forceful statements from senior management and the Board and by the Bank's willingness to increase staffing for gender work. The study included recommendations aimed at improving the Bank's capacity to respond to this increased level of support (Box 5.1).

The President has firmly established his commitment to integrating gender in ESW and lending and to broadening the Bank's dialogue with borrowers, other agencies, and NGOs to include gender issues. His speech at the 1996 Annual Meetings showed this clearly. Since the Beijing conference, senior managers have frequently expressed their own support for mainstreaming gender, most recently during a gender symposium for Asia. A gender committee reporting to the President and an expert advisory group are in place, each having met once.

Many encouraging steps have been taken at the regional level. The regional offices are completing their gender action plans, which were initiated shortly after the Beijing conference. The plans place a strong emphasis on reviewing gender aspects at the country level (through ESW and gender-specific reviews) and on integrating the findings into a substantive discussion of gender issues and priorities in the CASs. Gender specialists now work at the resident missions in Bangladesh, India, Indonesia, and Pakistan, as well as in Peru. Staff have been nominated as "gender focal points" in all country departments in AFR and Asia. The Gender and Poverty Team set up in the Asia

Technical Department to provide support to the two Asia regions has been able to function effectively by leveraging its small budget with trust funds, and by decentralizing support on gender in the country departments and the field offices. The team has produced useful country gender profiles, and it is completing a tool kit on micro-finance in collaboration with the Consultative Group to Assist the Poorest and the Agriculture Department. ECA, MNA, and LAC also have nominated several contact persons in addition to their regional coordinator. In AFR as in LAC, the work of the NGO liaison officers has provided opportunities for increased attention to gender issues. But there have also been some negative developments. The new assignments are in addition to a full work program, and few incremental resources, or none at all, have been allocated. The strong gender team established in the technical department to serve Africa had been actively supported in the early 1990s by regional managers, and the team was able to draw from trust funds to cover dissemination work and consultant positions. Yet in the past two years, the team has been reduced to part of one position as dedicated trust funds are exhausted.

In the center, the Gender Analysis and Policy Team (GAP) has provided guidance and technical support to the regions for policy and sector work as well as for lending. Drawing from the experience of previous years, GAP has worked with each region to develop seminars and training workshops that focus specifically on gender concerns at the regional level, most recently in MNA and the two Asia regions. GAP has worked with the Training Department and the Leadership and Learning Center to integrate gender issues into training courses on traditional sectors and disciplines. Tool kits have been issued for the agriculture and the water and sanitation sectors, together with visual material Bank staff can use to help sensitize their borrower counterparts to gender issues. Available sources of funding have also been used successfully for gender-related preparation work, including the Institutional Development Fund; the Country Operations Support Fund, managed by the Asia Gender and Poverty team for the two Asia regions; and a special WID fund in MNA and ECA. Bank management reports that about half of FIAHS-supported operations include some attempts to incorporate gender issues into the proposed work and that the presence of social scientists hired with FIAHS funding has led to increased attention to gender. OED has found that FIAHS funds have been used for gender-related work even more frequently than management has acknowledged.

Looking ahead

To better understand the factors that contributed to the positive changes noted in chapters 3 and 4, OED organized two sets of focus group discussions.[2] Technical staff in the central vice presidencies and the regions responsible for providing policy and technical guidance to task managers identified the characteristics of a Bank in which gender would be mainstreamed (Box 5.2). Separately, task managers who had achieved excellent gender integration in a project or in nonlending work approved in FY94 and FY95 identified numerous factors that facilitated or hampered their efforts. Using their experience as a guide, OED identified four elements essential to integrating gender into Bank work (Box 5.3).

The responses of the two groups parallel the findings of the OED reviews. The 1994 study showed that the Bank had shifted from a reactive to a proactive stance on gender when senior management and the Board made clear to staff and borrowers their commitment to addressing these issues. The fo-

Box 5.2: What the Bank would look like if gender were mainstreamed: the views of gender practitioners

1. A clear strategy, with goals and targets, would be in place to implement the Bank's gender policy; all levels of management would actively support the strategy.

Top management would send a clear, consistent message to borrowers and staff that gender is important for development effectiveness and should be an integral part of country-focused analysis. Management would set specific goals and minimum standards. One practitioner said that in the truly mainstreamed Bank, a "clear-cut, articulated policy for achieving gender goals has been framed and definite targets have been set."

2. Gender would be considered an integral part of analytical work for economic and sector work, country strategy, and lending work; interventions would be planned to meet the needs of both men and women.

Country directors would ensure that gender is addressed in the country work program and would allocate resources accordingly. Country managers would be held accountable for carrying out the work program. As another participant noted, "Reporting on country activities must explicitly include the extent of attention to gender."

3. Staff would be aware of the relevance of gender issues for Bank work and would know enough to bring in technical support when needed.

Gender would be recognized by all staff as an issue of efficiency as well as equity. Staff, especially the country teams, would receive guidance and technical support from gender practitioners with formal responsibilities for contributing state-of-the-art knowledge on gender issues in Bank work. The Bank budget would allocate funds to meet gender concerns.

4. An institutional framework would be designed to support mainstreaming.

Country teams, not just staff working specifically on gender, would be given incentives to carry out gender-related actions and would be held accountable. The country teams would be the focal point for systematic efforts to raise awareness of gender issues, for training tailored to specific needs, and for information dissemination and cross-region exchanges. "It is important to penetrate the country team," a practitioner pointed out.

cus group participants applauded the renewed commitment to gender that senior management has demonstrated in the last 18 months, although they agreed this commitment was not uniform across all levels of management.

But they also agreed that while leadership is necessary, in itself it is not enough to promote the changes mainstreaming gender requires. Success will depend on a comprehensive institutional knowledge of what works and what does not. It also needs appropriate skills, institutional support, and resources. During the focus groups, task managers and technical staff frequently cited the high-quality research on gender completed in recent years. But they insisted that many task managers, while willing to address gender concerns, do not feel knowledgeable enough to handle them or even to bring in the appropriate expertise.

Box 5.3: What I need to integrate gender into my work: the views of task managers

1. All parties, especially Bank managers, must be openly committed to achieving gender objectives. Borrowers must be aware of and willing to address the issues.

Support from Bank management was seen as instrumental in integrating gender into economic and sector work and projects. "Management gave [the issue] a high profile in the dialogue with the client—it was on the agenda at the donor consortium meeting," said one manager. "This gave a strong message to our clients, to Bank staff, and to other donors." Another observed, "The biggest factor was a clear signal from Bank management to the client country and other donors that attention to gender issues was a critical factor in our relationship with them."

Participants' experience with resource allocation in terms of staff time and funding varied. "This [gender] was a major part of my work program—that is, I had the incentives to do it well and was given credit for good output," said one. Others cited resource constraints, the problem of "having to do it in one's spare time," and lack of support from managers and other Bank staff who "think... that gender issues are not serious development issues."

2. A sufficient body of knowledge of gender-related issues in the country must be available, and it must be applied in the framework of relevant research results.

Bank staff should draw from all available knowledge sources, from the latest research to local work and the experience of development agencies and universities. One participant noted, "We were able to tap into a network of university-based ethnographers and anthropologists (based in the United States) with a lot of experience in thinking about gender issues as they relate to classroom behaviors. This turned out to be surprisingly applicable to the rural Third World context we were working in." Participants mentioned as positive factors the "rigorously analyzed evidence" of the high return to educating girls and the fact that high-level managers have publicly promoted this evidence.

3. Bank teams must have adequate skills in handling gender issues, as well as easy access to practical examples of successful projects.

Although the participating task managers were arguably among the most experienced and competent to integrate gender aspects in their work, they felt uncertain when it came to working with gender issues "on the ground." They called for more information on experience relevant to their work, wider dissemination of field-tested methods and techniques, and increased training opportunities. They also emphasized the need for strong social expertise in both Bank and borrower teams.

4. Innovative approaches should be tested and piloted under local conditions.

Good design and implementation of gender-related objectives build on a thorough knowledge of the local situation and an understanding of the points of view of different stakeholders. Several task managers described how a pilot phase enabled them to test innovative strategies and adapt these to the local situation in partnership with the stakeholders.

The focus group participants found that the current focus on country management has opened a potential avenue for country teams to increase their attention to gender and expand the dialogue with borrowers. They emphasized that current efforts to improve the quality of the CAS papers *"could be a great instrument to mainstream gender if adequately followed up."* But they also cautioned that adequate incentives and clear lines of accountability must be set. They concluded that while progress is being made, gender is not yet mainstreamed. The participants were concerned that proposed institutional changes might put this progress at risk.

The Bank's Committee on Development Effectiveness reaffirmed that gender issues are economic and social issues, not just women's issues

On July 1, 1996, staff working on gender[3] briefed CODE on the implementation of the Bank's gender policy. Staff reported that "progress has been made...but gender issues are still far from being successfully integrated in all the Bank's work."[4] Staff explained that each region was finalizing a gender action plan. Bank management and regional representatives also expressed concern that efforts to mainstream gender remain vulnerable and could be curtailed under the new Bank structure and processes. Yet, a cross-cutting issue such as gender is relevant to all networks and sectors, and mechanisms are needed to draw on potential synergies across countries and sectors.

Participants in the focus groups emphasized that gender continues to need "champions" in the networks and regions—managers and staff who are formally assigned to promote and guide work on gender issues and are evaluated in part on their work in this area. In recent weeks, management has agreed that the poverty reduction and economic management network (PREM) will include families on poverty and on gender.[5] PREM is an appropriate "home" for leadership on gender, as long as the skills of social scientists are recognized as integral to gender analysis and systematic links to other networks and to regional offices are established.

Conclusion

Following the July 1996 briefing described in the section above, CODE reaffirmed that gender issues are economic and social issues and not exclusively women's issues, and as such they permeate all aspects of the Bank's work. This update shows that some excellent work on gender issues is being done and that projects with gender-related actions are associated with satisfactory outcomes. Regional offices have produced a flurry of ideas and innovative initiatives. Gender action plans are being completed, and the social action plans include gender. The high standards and commitment of many staff, both those who work explicitly on gender issues and task managers, are exemplary. But the integration of gender concerns into Bank work is not yet systematic.

The summary of this study presents detailed recommendations. Generally, the current emphasis on portfolio management at the country level and on technical excellence through "networks" opens a window of opportunity. So do ongoing efforts in the Bank to better document development progress through performance indicators, to understand the social dimensions of development through social assessments, and to involve stakeholders in decisions that affect their lives. In order to be effective, each of these efforts should include gender concerns. Success requires a coherent strategy at all levels of management and a realistic understanding of the skills and resources needed to integrate gender issues into Bank work.

Notes

1. Draft dated October 10, 1996, based on the Development Assistance Committee report presented in Beijing.
2. A total of 115 staff were invited to contribute, and 43 did so. The focus groups used the groupware technology, alternating between individual inputs from each participant and group discussion, in order to document individual experiences and identify points of consensus and disagreement within the groups. Two sessions were held with task managers and one with gender technical staff.
3. The Gender Analysis and Policy Group team in the Poverty and Social Policy Department, Human Capacity Development, and gender coordinators in each region.
4. Progress in Mainstreaming Gender into World Bank Work, note prepared for the Committee on Development Effectiveness meeting of May 17, 1996 (postponed to July 1, 1996).
5. This is similar to the current Poverty and Social Policy Department, except that staff with coordination responsibilities on nongovernmental organizations and participation will move to the Social Development Family of the Environmentally and Socially Sustainable Development Network.

Annex: Study methodology

This report updates the conclusions of the 1994 Operations Evaluation Department (OED) study (published in 1995; see Murphy 1995) in light of the evidence gained since the study was completed. The regions and management have reported on their implementation of the OED recommendations made in 1994, and they briefed the Committee on Development Effectiveness on progress in FY96. In addition to this documentation, the update draws principally from work in the following areas:

- Update of the database, created for the 1994 study, of investment projects approved since FY67 and found to include some type of gender-related action. The original database included 615 projects approved from FY67–93. The database now includes the years FY94–96, with a total of 802 projects. Of these 802, 254 are completed and have been rated for project achievements (in an implementation completion report [ICR] if not through an OED review).

- Analysis of implementation and results for the 58 projects with gender-related action, approved in FY87 or since, completed by December 1995, and for which a project completion report (PCR) or ICR could be obtained by August 15, 1996 (at least in draft). Project documents and files were reviewed, together with midterm evaluations and completion report.

- Review of sector work focused specifically on gender issues (women in development [WID] assessments had been reviewed for the 1994 study), as well as poverty assessments and country assistance strategy papers for the 12 countries with the greatest gap between men and women on key health and education indicators.

- Focus groups with task managers who included particularly good attention to gender issues in their projects and sector work, and with staff responsible for promoting attention to gender in the regions and central vice-presidencies. A total of 43 staff participated.

Sources of data

The 1994 database of 615 projects with some type of gender-related action had been compiled from the Bank's management information system, notes from the first WID advisor, a database created by the first WID division with projects approved starting in FY88, and reviews of annual reports, world development reports, and internal reports. For projects approved from FY94–96, a list of projects with gender-related action was obtained from the Gender Analysis and Policy team (GAP). In all cases, OED reviewed the project objectives to confirm the presence of some gender-related action. The percentages of projects with gender-related action in this report differ slightly from those given in earlier Women in Development Division, Population and Human Resources Department (PHRWD), or GAP progress reports, for two reasons. First, since practically all projects with gender-related action are investment projects, OED calculated percentages against all investment projects only, while PHRWD gave percentages of projects with gender-related action against all lending operations. Second, PHRWD made a few corrections in its database after some of its early reports were issued. After further checks by OED, a few more errors (project duplication) were corrected, slightly lowering the total number of projects with gender-related action for FY88–93. For projects approved in FY94–96, the OED review confirmed all rating given by GAP.

Review and analysis of completed projects

The 1994 study evaluated the implementation experience and gender achievements for two clusters of projects with gender-related action: (a) an "old cluster" of the 36 projects cited in World Bank 1979; and (2) a "new cluster" of 24 projects approved in FY87–88 and expected to be completed by June 1994. Surprisingly, 8 of these 24 projects were still not completed in June 1995, although they had been scheduled for closing before or on June 1994 at the time of the study.

For the update report, the characteristics and achievements of completed projects are discussed on the basis of a larger cluster of 58 projects with gender-related action: all such projects approved in FY87 or later, closed by December 1995, and for which a PCR or ICR could be obtained, even in draft form, by August 15, 1996. This cluster combines 16 of the projects already discussed in the new cluster of the 1994 study, albeit with more evidence of results, together with an additional 42 projects. In each case, the most recent rating of outcomes, sustainability, and institutional development impact was used, that is, audit or OED rating on the basis of an ICR review, or the ICR itself. In the update, the analysis is limited to projects that are actually completed, rather than within six months of expected completion, partly because of the delayed closings observed for the 1994 new cluster, and partly so evaluation ratings would be available for all these completed projects.

The review focused on the implementation experience and actual achievements of the gender-related actions objectives, the quality of their supervision, and generally their incorporation in the overall project implementation and achievements. All documents from staff appraisal reports (SAR) to ICRs or audits were reviewed, together with the project files and supervision reports, using a standard questionnaire revised in light of the 1994 findings. Achievements of the gender-related actions were rated against their stated objectives, and quality of supervision was assessed through evidence of attention to gender issues in supervision reports or aide-memoires. A matrix was built around the key factors that could affect implementation.

Logit analysis

A logit analysis was done to assess whether various variables made achievement of gender objectives in these 58 projects more likely. Univariate analyses show that gender achievement is lower in the Africa regional office (but a weak relationship only—see the end of this section for further explanation) and higher in the human resources sector. There was no relationship with the source of funding (International Development Association [IDA]/ International Bank for Reconstruction and Development) nor with the countries' income.

All projects that achieved their gender objectives were rated satisfactory. Positive correlations were also found between sustainability and gender achievement, and between institutional development and gender achievement. A relationship noted between time period and gender achievement (recent projects being more likely to achieve their gender objectives) could be due to the higher concentration of human resources projects in the more recent projects or to the known fact that delayed completion often signals implementation difficulties.

In order to determine which factor(s) seemed correlated to achievement of gender objectives, an unconditional logistic regression analysis was done. The outcome variables were defined as gender achievement score of "2" or higher versus "0" or "1." The explanatory variables were as follows: fiscal year of approval of the project, amount of loan in nearest million dollars, income level of country, any IDA component to the loan, region, agricultural, human resource or other sector, sustainability, institutional development, and outcome scores as based upon the OED rating schemes, gender analysis, supervision of the gender component, integration of the gender objective into the main project objectives, and supervision of the gender component.

Variables were analyzed in a logistic regression model. The EGRET software model was used, and tested for significance to a two-sided p value of 5 percent. Each explanatory variable was examined in the model singularly, and then a baseline model consisting of year, amount, income level and IDA lending was established. To this baseline model, individual variables which were significant in univariate analyses were examined individually. These were Africa or other region; human resource or other sector; outcome, sustainability, and institutional development scores; and integration of the gender objectives into the main objective. Finally the last model included all variables from the baseline model and the significant explanatory variables. The latter may be unreliable due to the small sample size and co-linearity of some of the explanatory variables. For each analysis, we produced two sided p values, beta-coefficients, and an overall goodness of fit, as measured by deviance on the appropriate degrees of freedom. Any missing values were omitted from the analyses.

Review of design quality in 120 projects approved in FY94–95

The SAR and president's report for all projects with gender-related action approved in those two years were reviewed, together with any supervision documentation already available. The 1994 questionnaire was used (with some revisions). The reviewer assigned ratings for the presence and quality of gender analysis, presence and level of participatory approaches during design or implementation, and integration of gender objectives into project objectives. Staff (and in a few cases consultants) involved were frequently interviewed for further information and to understand the context in which some design decisions were made.

Focus group discussions with successful task managers and gender coordinators

The OED reviews of selected sector work and of design quality in projects approved in FY94 and FY95, together with information provided by the regional coordinators, led to the identification of 85 operations (mostly projects, with a few economic and sector work [ESW]) with good attention to gender aspects in their design. The task managers for these projects were invited to two focus group discussions. The enthusiasm with which most of the invitees reacted, even though many were or would be on mission at the proposed dates, shows a need for recognition that their work is worthwhile and a strong desire to help change Bank practices. Twenty-three task managers participated in two groupware sessions; another eight contributed comments and additions to the draft summary of the two focus group discussions.

The task managers were asked to list individually factors that facilitated or hampered the integration of gender issues in the ESW or project for which they were selected. In the next step, the groups organized their lists into logical categories. Finally, the participants were asked to draw an action plan through which the Bank could act on the factors under its control, or could promote attention to gender in its dialogue with the borrowers.

Because task managers raised a number of institutional issues, another round of focus groups was organized with staff who have a formal assignment (full or part time) to promote attention to gender in their region or sector, as well as all members of the central GAP. Twenty-seven staff were invited, nine participated, and another four provided their views individually. The participants were asked to identify what evidence would demonstrate that gender was being mainstreamed in line with gender policy. They were then asked to assess the Bank's strengths and weaknesses against the standard thus established and to identify actions that would accelerate the pace of mainstreaming.

Bibliography

Bennett, Lynn, M. Goldberg, and P. Hunte. 1996. "Ownership and Sustainability: Lessons on Group-Based Financial Services from South Asia." In L. Bennett and C. Cuevas, eds., *Journal of International Development*, 8(8):271–88. New York: Wiley Publisher.

Cagatay, Nilufer, Diane Elson, and Caren Grown, eds. 1995. *World Development, Gender, Adjustment, and Macroeconomics* 23(11). Great Britain: Nuffield Press, Ltd.

Fong, Monica. 1993. *The Role of Women in Rebuilding the Russian Economy.* Studies of Economics in Transformation Paper 10. Washington, D.C.: World Bank.

Fong, Monica S., and Anjana Bhushan. 1996. *Toolkit on Gender in Agriculture.* Gender Toolkit Series No. 1. Washington, D.C.: World Bank.

Fong, Monica S., Wendy Wakeman, and Anjana Bhushan. 1996. *Toolkit on Gender in Water and Sanitation.* Gender Toolkit Series No. 2. Washington, D.C.: World Bank.

IFPRI (International Food Policy Research Institute). 1995. *Women: The Key to Food Security.* Food Policy Report. Washington, D.C.: IFPRI.

Mahajan, V., and B.G. Ramola. 1996. "Financial Services for the Rural Poor and Women in India: Access and Sustainability." In L. Bennett and C. Cuevas, eds., *Journal of International Development* 8(8):211–24. New York: Wiley Publisher.

Malmberg-Calvo, Christina. 1994. "Case Study on the Role of Women in Rural Transport: Access of Women to Domestic Facilities." SSATP Working Paper 11, Africa Region. World Bank, Washington, D.C.

Moser, Caroline. 1996. *Confronting Crisis: A Summary of Household Responses to Poverty and Vulnerability in Four Poor Urban Communities.* Report 15462. Washington, D.C.: World Bank.

Murphy, J. 1995. *Gender Issues in World Bank Lending.* A World Bank Operations Evaluation Study. Washington, D.C.: World Bank.

Narayan, Deepa. 1995. *The Contribution of People's Participation: Evidence from 121 Rural Water Supply Projects.* ESD Occasional Paper 1. Washington, D.C.: World Bank.

Odaga, Adhiambo, and Ward Heneveld. 1995. *Girls and Schools in Sub-Saharan Africa: From Analysis to Action.* World Bank Technical Paper 298. Washington, D.C.: World Bank.

Reines, Sheila. 1995. "UN Women's Conferences and Women in the Bank." In World Bank, *Bank's World Magazine* 14(9). Washington, D.C.

Sivard, Ruth Leger. 1995. *Women...a world survey.* Washington, D.C.: World Priorities.

United Nations. 1995. *The World's Women 1995—Trends and Statistics.* New York: United Nations.

World Bank. 1979. *Recognizing the "Invisible" Woman in Development: The World Bank's Experience.* Washington, D.C.: World Bank.

———. 1994. *Poverty in Colombia.* World Bank Country Study. Washington, D.C.: World Bank.

———. 1995a. *Advancing Gender Equality: From Concept to Action.* Washington, D.C.: World Bank.

———. 1995b. "El Salvador—Moving to a Gender Approach: Issues and Recommendations." Sector Report 14407. World Bank, Washington, D.C.

———. 1995c. "Rural Women in the Sahel and their Access to Agricultural Extension." Sector Study 13532. World Bank, Washington, D.C.

———. 1995d. *The World Bank and Gender in India.* New Delhi: World Bank.

———. 1995e. *Toward Gender Equality: The Role of Public Policy.* Washington, D.C.: World Bank.

———. 1995f. *Understanding Poverty in Poland.* Country Study. Washington, D.C.: World Bank.

———. 1995g. *World Bank Participation Sourcebook.* Washington, D.C.: World Bank.

———. 1995h. *World Development Report: Workers in an Integrating World.* New York: Oxford University Press.

———. 1996a. *Improving Women's Health in India.* Development in Practice Book. Washington, D.C.: World Bank.

———. 1996b. "Togo: Overcoming the Crisis, Overcoming Poverty: A World Bank Poverty Assessment." World Bank, Washington, D.C.

Supplement

Introductory note

Feedback of evaluation results within the World Bank

Each study by the Bank's independent Operations Evaluation Department is reviewed by the Bank's management before being discussed by a committee of the Board of Executive Directors. Management provides a detailed response to the recommendations outlined in the study. This response is discussed by the committee and, together with a record of actions promised and taken, is recorded in a "policy ledger" accessible to all Bank staff. The Bank's executive directors have requested that all published studies by the Operations Evaluation Department include a synopsis of the management response and the committee's findings.

Management response

The OED update on Mainstreaming Gender in World Bank Lending is a valuable document that provides an overview of the Bank's past and current work in mainstreaming gender. It gives broad coverage to the treatment of gender issues in different sectors, and usefully identifies examples of both opportunities lost and those of good practice, thus providing useful lessons on what approaches and policies have been successful.

The report uses a number of innovative new data sources for its information, including focus group discussions with task managers and gender coordinators, and a logit analysis. These contribute to the richness of the study.

As the report states, improvements in mainstreaming gender could not have been achieved without the support and commitment of all levels of Bank management. The report rightly recognizes that continued support and commitment will be necessary to push this work forward, especially given the upcoming move towards the network structure, as well as the regional reorganizations. Management will revisit the recently completed Regional Gender Action Plans, identify monitorable actions, and assign implementation and monitoring responsibilities according to the new structures.

Management supports the major OED recommendations.

Mainstreaming Gender in World Bank Lending: An Update
Ledger of OED recommendations
Management responses and actions

OED recommendations	*Management response*	*Actions promised*
Gender concerns should be fully addressed in social assessments, in the selection of performance indicators, and in ICRs.		
• The social development family should include in its forthcoming guidelines on social assessment a discussion of how to link gender analysis, stakeholder analysis, and social assessments;	• Agreed. The particular responsibility of the social development family will be not only social assessments, but also to ensure that gender is mainstreamed into all their "thematic areas." Gender analysis will be undertaken by all the networks and Regions.	• The social development family has already established a thematic group on gender and social development A high priority objective is to ensure that a coherent gender and social development framework is reflected in key Bank instruments and procedures, including the social assessment guidelines. • East Asia and South Asia have committed to conduct social assessments in a number of high risk/high social content projects over the next three years, which will include gender analysis.
• Regional staff and management with assistance from the Operations Policy Department (OPR) should ensure that the ongoing "retooling" of monitoring and evaluation indicators in the current portfolio (and especially in participation flagships and pilot projects) disaggregate data on men and women wherever appropriate; and	• Agreed. Performance indicator data should be disaggregated by gender, determined on a case by case basis. OPR consultants are providing technical assistance to the regions in the ongoing "retrofitting" of the portfolio, but regional management is responsible for the scope and adequacy of the indicators which are agreed to with Borrowers.	• Performance indicator data will be disaggregated by gender where appropriate and agreed with Borrowers. • The networks will, in conjunction with the regions, develop gender-related performance indicators across all sectors and make sure that staff are trained on how to identify and use them. These indicators should not only be used in ICRs and project documents but in ESW as well, as gender considerations are often relevant in the analysis of macroeconomic, infrastructure and financial issues.
• OPR should stipulate in the ICR guidelines (OP 13.55, currently being updated) that ICRs systematically check for and document results separately for men and women, when data are	• Agreed. A reference to gender would be included in OP 13.55 (which is expected to be updated in FY98), along with other changes in the guidelines. Reference to gender is included in OPs/BPs already	• Updated ICR guidelines will include a reference to gender and ask for a discussion of results by gender where appropriate and when data is available.

OED recommendations	*Management response*	*Actions promised*
available, whether the project included some gender-related action or not.	revised. Nevertheless, imposing a requirement "that ICRs systematically check for and document results separately by gender ... whether the project included gender-related action or not" is too rigid. First, in its current approach to operational policy formulation, management is trying to keep specific new requirements to a core minimum, in order to leave the key judgments to regional staff and management. Secondly, although the recommendation does say "when data are available," there is a concern about the incremental cost of collecting the data when not available or of dubious added value (for example, when the gender is obvious without collecting data, as in a project on prenatal care). While in principle, management supports this recommendation, in practice, data limitations may dictate cost-benefit tradeoffs.	
The Office of the Senior Vice President and Chief Economist should advance the state of knowledge on gender issues by setting up a systematic program of research to examine the gender impact of project lending and policy reform. • The research program should explicitly address both quantitative and qualitative dimensions of gender and should focus on both micro- and macro-level issues.	• Agreed. A gender-focused research program needs to be carried out in conjunction with PREM and the regions, in order to have operational significance. It will be essential to build this program based on existing data collection and monitoring systems in order to avoid duplication and overburdening task teams • The recommendation is consistent with the preparatory work that would be required to ensure	• The planned research program to be undertaken by the Gender Family in PREM, with DEC and regional collaboration will include research on gender inequality and growth; on the gender dimensions of poverty measurement; and on gender and intrahousehold analysis. In all these areas, there will be an explicit integration of qualitative analysis to the quantitative methodology.

OED recommendations	*Management response*	*Actions promised*
	that the gender dimensions of poverty are adequately addressed in the WDR on poverty envisioned for 2000.	• Relevant input, output, outcome and impact indicators will be developed to facilitate a systematic program of research to examine the gender impact of project lending and policy reform. Several regions will be developing their own data collection and monitoring systems during FY97, to become operational during FY98.
• To support such research will require that appropriate gender-disaggregated data be collected routinely, not only through projects but also through household survey instruments such as the Living Standard**[s]** Measurement Surveys.	• Agreed. LSMS and other surveys should routinely collect gender-disaggregated data. In fact, LSMS surveys already do this for health, nutrition, fertility, migration, education and employment. The importance of gender disaggregated data collection cannot be overemphasized, as it is an effective tool to bring gender issues to light both for Governments and for the Bank.	• Part of the ongoing review of the LSMS in DEC includes support for when and how to collect gender disaggregated data on other topics. The LAC region is taking initiatives to bring a clearer gender perspective and to include more gender-specific questions in the LSMS as part of the ongoing joint IDB/Bank initiative to improve LSMS in selected countries.
• This research should be undertaken in consultation with all networks and OED.	• Agreed.	• The Gender Family Sector Board will consist of representatives of all regions and networks, thus ensuring that research programs are decided through joint consultation. OED will be consulted.
Each region should establish which elements of their gender action plans will be implemented within the next 36 months, establish time-bound, monitorable targets, and assign responsibility for monitoring implementation progress. The poverty reduction and economic management (PREM) network, working with the Regions, should ensure that institution-wide progress is monitored.	• Agreed. Even though regional gender action plans vary across the Bank in terms of ownership and scope, the establishment of targets for regional gender action plans is fully supported.	• Matrices with clearer time-bound actions will be prepared for all regional gender action plans (RGAPs) translating their recommendations into work programs and budget allocations that can be monitored. The RGAPs will need to be adapted after the new network structures and regional reorganizations are completed, and clear accountabilities for implementation and monitoring according to the new structures will be assigned. • The Africa Region has integrated monitoring and reporting responsibilities into the work pro-

OED recommendations	*Management response*	*Actions promised*
		gram of focal points on gender in each country team. Overall RGAP implementation monitoring will be centralized at the regional level through the Regional Gender Coordinator, and this reporting will be integrated into Bankwide reporting via the PREM network. Other regions will clarify these responsibilities after regional reorganizations are completed.
The network councils should ensure that each network and family takes steps to mainstream gender as appropriate in its work, and, where possible, specify priority goals and targets. The proposed PREM gender family should make promoting synergistic interactions across the institution one of its priorities.	• Agreed. Where appropriate, the networks are taking steps to mainstream gender concerns. For example, in HD, girls' education and women's health are priority issues; in ESSD, a thematic group on gender gives explicit attention to gender issues.	• The structure of the Gender Family Sector Board, with representation of all networks and regions, will ensure continuous interaction and synergy among all regions and networks on mainstreaming gender issues.

Summary of Committee on Development Effectiveness findings

The Committee on Development Effectiveness (CODE) welcomed the report's important findings that projects with gender-related actions achieved their overall objectives in relatively greater proportion than did projects similar in sector and year of approval but without gender actions, and that projects that explicitly incorporate gender goals into their main objectives are the most likely to achieve their gender objectives. The study also found that although the design quality of gender-related actions improved significantly, there is still substantial room for increasing the proportion of projects and country assistance strategies (CASs) that systematically address gender issues. The committee endorsed OED's recommendations and expressed satisfaction that the response from management confirmed a commitment to achieving the objective of mainstreaming gender in Bank work. The committee reiterated the need for gender to be treated as both an economic and a social issue. It stressed that the social development family should include, in its forthcoming guidelines on social assessment, a discussion of how to link gender analysis, stakeholder analysis, and social assessments. The committee emphasized the importance of carrying out gender-based analysis at the beginning of the project cycle. It welcomed the progress made in developing and implementing regional gender action plans. The committee underscored the need to advance the state of knowledge on gender issues by improving data collection and analysis. It welcomed management's response that the planned research program to be undertaken by the gender family in the Poverty Reduction and Economic Management network, with the collaboration of the Office of Development Economics and Chief Economist and the regions, will include research on gender inequality and growth; on the dimensions of poverty measurement; and on gender and intrahousehold analysis. Finally, the committee stressed that it expects the current momentum in mainstreaming gender in World Bank lending to continue, and it looks forward to receiving interim progress reports on this subject.